Sue Sharpe, in her invaluable book, young mothers, both black and whit backgrounds and circumstances to changed worlds. Young motherho fast, with little freedom or money and a lot of responsibility, but it often adds invaluable love and meaning to girls' lives. *Falling for Love* looks sensitively and sympathetically at teenage motherhood and all its implications – relations with parents, education, living alone, Mother and Baby Homes, adoption and much else; it strikes many familiar chords, and shows how easily this could happen to any girl.

Sue Sharpe was born in London in 1945. After studying psychology, sociology and philosophy at Leicester University, she returned to London in 1968 to do an MSc course in Social Psychology at the London School of Economics. There she carried out research for a thesis on the expectations of teenage girls in London secondary schools, which formed the basis of her book on the development of sex roles, *Just Like a Girl*. This led to an increasing interest in women and work and her next book, *Double Identity*, focused on the lives of working mothers. She became involved in the Women's Liberation Movement in the early 1970s and has worked in various areas of feminist research and teaching. In 1980 she spent sixteen months living and travelling in Mexico and Central America. Since then she has worked mainly freelance, interviewing and writing for a variety of books and magazines, and working as a part-time researcher at the Middlesex Hospital. She lives in East London.

Virago Upstarts is a new series of books for girls and young women. Upstarts are about love and romance, family and friends, work and school – and about new preoccupations – because in the last two decades the lives and expectations of girls have changed a lot. With fiction of all kinds – humour, mystery, love stories, science fiction, detective, thrillers – and nonfiction, this new series will show the funny, difficult, and exciting real lives and times of teenage girls in the 1980s. Lively, down-to-earth and entertaining, Virago's new list is an important new Upstart on the scene.

FALLING FOR LOVE

Teenage Mothers Talk

SUE SHARPE

VIRAGO UPSTARTS

Published by VIRAGO PRESS Limited 1987
41 William IV Street, London WC2N 4DB

Copyright © Sue Sharpe 1987

British Library Cataloguing in Publication Data
Sharpe, Sue
    Falling for love: teenage mothers talk.
    —(Virago upstarts)
    1. Adolescent mothers
    I. Title
    306.8'743   HQ759.4

    ISBN 0-86068-841-0

Typeset by Florencetype Ltd of Kewstoke, Avon
Printed in Great Britain by Cox & Wyman Ltd of
Reading, Berkshire

CONTENTS

ACKNOWLEDGEMENTS

First and foremost I would like to thank all the teenage mothers and pregnant teenagers from around the country who have shared their personal experiences, thoughts and feelings in this book, both those who wrote to me, and those who I also met and talked with. Each of them has contributed a valuable part to a fuller understanding of teenage motherhood. During my travels I also went to visit several projects organised for pregnant teenagers and teenage mothers and enjoyed meeting and talking with both the workers and the girls involved. In particular I would like to thank Hilary Cozens, Monica Furlong, and Yvonne Ford, from the Arbour project in Liverpool; Lesley Horton, from the Barkerend Unit in Bradford; Glynis Francis, from the Manchester Youth and Community Services Young Women's Project; Miss K.M. Leigh from the Midwifery Department of Wythenshawe Hospital, Manchester, and the midwives and physiotherapist running the hospital's Teenage Parents Club; and Mrs J.P. Reid from Beacon Lodge Mother and Baby Home. I am grateful to many other people who helped me in various ways, some by introducing me to teenage mothers, and others by giving me useful information and contacts in the early stages, especially Jeremy Bennett, Chris Ellis, and Carol Fardoe. The magazines *Just Seventeen*, *Mizz*, and *19* were also very helpful in allowing me to contact teenage mothers through their pages. Thanks also to those who provided me with transport or places to stay when I was travelling round the country, and to those who transcribed my many tapes, especially Sonia Lane; and a special word of appreciation to John Freeman for his generous help and encouragement, and to the friends who had to put up with my working nonstop to get the manuscript completed in time.

INTRODUCTION

It's funny, when I read your notice in the magazine, I turned the page and I thought, wait a minute, I'm a teenage mother. It's quite strange because when you think of teenage mothers you think of Michelle in *Eastenders* having all those problems and the father running off and everythng. I don't think of myself like that. I'm lucky it's worked out quite differently for me.   (Julie, aged eighteen with a nine-month-old daughter)

Unlike Michelle in *Eastenders*, my situation was quite different as I was going out with the father of my son. But in the nine months of carrying my child, the feelings and reactions of Michelle's were very much the same as my own. (Teresa, aged nineteen, with a three-year-old son)

When Michelle got pregnant at sixteen in the television series *Eastenders*, she brought the situation of teenage mothers to the attention of the nation. Millions of viewers became aware of some of the practical and emotional problems and watched as she struggled to bring up a baby without a partner or an income. Many of the young mothers contributing to this book would identify with a lot of her responses and feelings.

Society tends to ignore the inherent sexuality of younger teenagers, especially girls, preferring to see them as innocent children, so consequently when girls do fall pregnant, they have few rights or benefits as mothers. Adolescence is accepted as a time to explore and experiment and find some sense of identity, and yet when this includes sexuality it is condemned and denied. Those who have become pregnant are treated as children who have made mistakes, and who are assumed to make inadequate mothers, which is patronising and wrong. However unintended the pregnancy was, if a girl decides to keep the baby for whatever reason, she is becoming a mother with all its attendant responsibilities. She deserves to be treated with respect and sensitivity, and to be formally recognised.

Everyone's life is different, and so I wanted to hear from as wide a variety of teenage mothers as I could. I wrote in several magazines asking girls to share their experiences of pregnancy and motherhood with me, and received a tremendous response. I got letters from all over the country, from young mothers of all ages and circumstances. Several more were contacted through teachers and other sources, and I also asked some older teenage mothers to write about their earlier years. Subsequently I travelled to many parts of Britain and met over thirty girls, mainly in their homes with their children. They made me welcome and gave up their time to talk freely and openly about everything that had happened to them. I really enjoyed our conversations and feel privileged to have shared their very personal experiences. Their voices can be heard throughout the following pages, where I refer to them consistently by name. All their names, however, have been changed to preserve their anonymity.

Becoming pregnant and having a baby changes your life completely, whatever your age. For younger mothers it usually comes as a surprise, an unintended consequence of a past or current sexual relationship, and an event for which there has been little planning or preparation. Many of the things that may happen to you if you are young, pregnant and choose to keep your baby, are described by the girls talking here. Their experiences and feelings embrace lots of important areas of life – love, boyfriends, sex and contraception; relationships with parents and friends; school, adoption, abortion, pregnancy and birth, Mother and Baby Homes, surviving on social security benefits, living alone, getting married, and much more. Each chapter of the book concentrates on a specific area, which is illustrated by the lives of several mothers who have had particularly relevant experiences.

It's not difficult to get pregnant, as many young girls have discovered, but nowadays the options have changed. It is easier now to prevent pregnancy through contraception, and to terminate it through abortion. Although it is a subject often exploited by the media, teenage motherhood has in fact been decreasing. It fell in the 1970s and early 1980s while the abortion rate was rising.[1] This fall in pregnancy rate has been explained by the greater use of contraceptives by teenagers, particularly those over sixteen. The proportion of younger mothers (under sixteen) is very small compared to the total number of teenage mothers, and this applies to other countries such as Australia, New Zealand and Canada, as well as to Britain.[2] However, there is evidence of a slight increase in teenage pregnancy rate in 1984 in England and Wales for all ages between fourteen and nineteen compared to the previous year, with a consequent rise in the numbers of girls who had babies and who had abortions.[3] Teenage mothers are not a significantly large group, nor are they a particularly increasing 'problem' in this country, but their lives are quite different to those of other girls of the same age without children. And as those talking in this book illustrate, what has happened to them can easily happen to any girl.

The teenage years cover a period in which young women and men mature physically, intellectually and emotionally. Therefore a fourteen-year-old teenage mother who is at school is in quite a different situation from a nineteen-year-old who may be working and married, and her pregnancy is usually viewed quite differently too. The majority of teenage mothers in Britain are eighteen or nineteen, but a significant number conceive below this age. The ages at which the mothers in this book became pregnant range from thirteen to eighteen, the majority between the ages of fourteen and seventeen. Many surveys divide teenagers into those over and those under sixteen, which is the official school leaving age. This often creates a confusion in estimating the number of schoolage mothers, as a sixteen-year-old can be counted both in the schoolage group and in the sixteen to nineteen-year-old group, depending on whether her birthday falls before or after the end of the school year.

Sixteen is a crucial age for teenage mothers. If you are under sixteen you are obliged to receive some kind of education until you reach this age. Not until sixteen can you legally marry, which means that all babies born to under sixteen-year-olds are inevitably illegitimate. It is also the age of consent for sexual intercourse, and therefore for a girl under this age to be pregnant is proof that an illegal act has taken place.[4] If this wasn't enough, the state does not recognise you as a mother until you are sixteen, when you are eligible to claim supplementary benefit, maternity grant and milk and vitamin tokens. (This has recently been changed in the new Social Security Act; before this, mothers under sixteen were entitled to maternity grant (£25) and milk and vitamin tokens.) This means that the cost of keeping a young mother and baby usually falls squarely on the family. All in all, being an under sixteen-year-old mother has little official recognised status at all, even though this involves the same care and costs as for an older mother.

The reasons why teenage girls get pregnant are many and various. Although a minority have wanted and planned

4

having a baby, most have not intended to get pregnant, at least not consciously. Some became pregnant through contraceptive failure, such as missing taking the Pill for a day, or a faulty condom, but most do it through not using any kind of contraception at all. While sexual activity amongst teenagers has increased, the use of contraception has lagged behind. Despite knowing about birth control, girls fail to go to the doctor or the clinic to get anything. Pregnancy often seems unreal, and something which will not happen to them. Sometimes the intention to go on the Pill is there, but it is put off until next week, or until their sixteenth birthday. When Victoria Gillick campaigned to prevent girls under sixteen getting contraceptive advice without their parents' consent, she created a lot of confusion, and although she was ultimately unsuccessful, many girls still assume that they cannot get the Pill or any other form of contraception, such as the cap or diaphragm, until this age.[5]

If you are in your late teens you may be very happy to be pregnant. Some older teenagers are married or in stable relationships within which having a baby is a wanted event. Some younger ones too may want children to fill some need for love and affection that may have been lacking in their lives. But on the whole, pregnancy comes as a surprise and a shock. The decision follows as to whether to have the baby or an abortion, assuming the pregnancy is made known early enough. Many pregnant teenagers delay making their pregnancy known until too many months have passed to do anything but have the baby. Sometimes they do not even realise they are pregnant. Adoption is another option, but is a less popular choice nowadays.

With the pregnancy confirmed, there are the reactions of boyfriends to deal with, assuming they are still around. Sometimes girls have already started another relationship by this time. Harder still, they have to tell their parents, whose reaction may be greatly feared. Sometimes parents are very upset and angry, but only very occasionally do they take the extreme course of making girls leave home. When they've got over the shock, most are mainly concerned for their daughters' welfare, and give them a lot of support, as illustrated many times in the accounts that follow.

Life is disrupted by having an abortion, but it is totally changed by having a baby. If girls are under sixteen, they can either continue at school, have a home tutor, or perhaps attend one of the few projects run specifically for pregnant schoolgirls and schoolgirl mothers, two of which – the Arbour Project in Liverpool and the Barkerend Unit in Bradford – are described here. They may for some reason go to a Mother and Baby Home for a short period before and after they have the baby, or even go to live with foster parents. Where to live is another question, and who to live with. Some get married, others live with their boyfriends, but a lot are on their own, and either return to the family home, or get a council flat or house. Having a baby usually means not being able to have a job as well so most young mothers have to make do with the various state benefits they are entitled to.

Although personal experiences vary a lot, teenage mothers in Britain tend to share certain similarities in their backgrounds. For instance, most girls come from lower income families – often one-parent families – and may be early school leavers.[6] This is not to say that middle-class girls don't get pregnant, they do, but they are more likely to be encouraged to use contraception, and also take the option of an abortion more than working-class girls. In working-class families it is not unusual for girls or boys to become parents at a relatively early age. Proportionally, quite a lot of black teenagers become pregnant too, and they may well have to contend with racism and discrimination in many areas of their lives.

It is quite common to find teenage mothers written about as people with certain medical and social problems. Emphasis is laid on the risks involved, the higher incidence of birth difficulties and subsequent infant illness, and the social difficulties encountered in coping with a baby, both emotionally and practically. Although these problems obviously exist, there are older mothers too who find it hard to cope with daily life. It is more often the poor conditions that many young mothers are forced to live in that negatively affect their lives, rather than simply their age or the experience of being a mother.

The mothers talking in this book are mainly in their mid to late teens, with children whose ages range from a few months to four years. The majority, both white and black, come from working-class backgrounds, a few have had a middle-class upbringing and education. Most of them are deeply committed to their children. Although having them has not made their lives any easier, they have got immense enjoyment from them and would not be without them. Looking back, they would have done a few things quite differently, but they certainly did not conform to the view taken by some authorities that they encountered, that they are children who have ruined their lives and wasted their education. They are now mothers with the responsibility for a child, and some of them would maintain that it is their baby that has given them the determination to do something more with their lives, however hard this may be. The years to come, as several older teenage mothers illustrate here, may confirm or contradict their current ideas and view, but it is the present that is important to them. It is usually they who made the choice to have and keep their babies, even though this does not always work out as happily or as easily as they may anticipate, and they deserve recognition and respect. I hope, as do the teenage mothers talking here, that this book will contribute to providing this.

> I think it's good to have a book on teenage mothers so other people can read it and see what others have gone through. I like to think I've been helpful to somebody else, so that they don't make the same mistake as I made, or so that they know the responsibilities they're taking on if they do have the baby. I wouldn't wish it upon anybody to get pregnant so young. Even though it's great having the baby, it's still a lot of hard work, especially when you are younger than usual. So I like to think I'm helping somebody else. (Bridget, aged sixteen)

I feel personally that the most difficult thing to cope with is not the physical and emotional changes I am going through but the attitudes of people around me. I have found the way I have been treated by qualified and unqualified people patronising and presumptuous and deeply offensive. The thing that makes this worse is that they really have meant well and were, I believe genuinely concerned. Their attitude, however, seemed to be that because I was young I was utterly unaware of what was happening to me, emotionally unstable, childish, and being forced into womanhood by a terrible mistake I had made.

I love my unborn baby deeply, just as I know other teenage mothers do. I do not consider he or she a terrible mistake which I will regret for the rest of my life, and I don't feel I have lost important years of my adolescence. I know that I have gained tremendously. Not only have I learned that soon I will not only be responsible for myself but a small vulnerable child who for many years to come will be under my protection, but I have also gained an inner strength that I never knew I was capable of having.

I hope your book will reveal a new and refreshing view on teenage pregnancy and motherhood. Perhaps changing some people's old and dated views so that soon when other young women undoubtedly become pregant they will be protected from what I personally find I am going through.   (Zoe, aged sixteen, and six months pregnant)

1
LOVE, BOYFRIENDS, SEX AND CONTRACEPTION

Today's teenagers have sex at a younger age than ever before. One recent study of teenage mothers[1] showed that two-thirds of these were already sexually experienced by the age of sixteen. Contrary to some people's beliefs, this does not imply an increase in casual sex and promiscuity. For most, there is an enduring search for bonds of love and loyalty, and other research showed that four out of five teenagers involved in a sexual relationship had been going out with their partner for six months or more.[2]

It is these teenage girls who more often fall pregnant, rather than those having more casual relationships, as the mothers in this book illustrate. Most of them had few or no sexual relationships before the father of their baby came along. This is not to deny that some young mothers do have short-term relationships and one-night stands, but the ones that get 'caught' are more often those who are in love and in a steady relationship. This may mean they have been going together for as little time as a few weeks, and a relationship of more than a month or two may be regarded as serious. Most of the mothers talking here had known their boyfriends for at least two months before they 'did it', and for almost two-thirds of them it was their first sexual relationship.

Love and romance are amongst the most important ingredients of life in these teenage years. Many hours may be spent daydreaming about meeting the ideal boyfriend and falling in love. At the beginning of a relationship sex is often taken for granted as a possibility, but girls have to take care that it does not happen too easily or too often. Being labelled a 'slag' or a 'sleep-around' is something that destroys a girl's reputation, and she often treads a fine line between being labelled as someone who does it or someone who doesn't[3] – 'if you do it you're a slag, if you don't you're a tight bitch.' One young mother, Folasade, implies that the distinction is implicit, 'Only true slags are slags. If you slept with a boy and he was your boyfriend, it didn't really matter.' If you are in love with someone, that makes it all right. In her girls' school, it was a bit like joining a club – 'girls who had on this side, and girls who hadn't on that side'. But in general, sleeping with your boyfriend is a relatively accepted thing.

For the majority of young mothers I talked to, it had been a mutual decision to have sex in the first place. For a few it was more their boyfriend's decision, and for two of them, the decision had been their own. In Denise's case, 'He didn't really know it was only his idea. I let him think it was mutual.' Some of them had found making love an enjoyable experience but others talked about how they had found sex an anti-climax, especially the first time. It hurt, they didn't feel anything much about it, and it was not at all the way they had thought it would be. Several thought sex was more important to men than to women. The effect of having a baby had also put some of them off sex altogether for a while, which is something that also happens to older mothers. But it seems sad that so many did not have a more enjoyable sexual introduction, especially when for a few it had been the one and only time. For Melanie, at fifteen, it had been her first sexual relationship, she now had a baby daughter and was still living with her family.

I didn't think much of the first time really. It wasn't how I imagined it. I thought you were supposed to enjoy it, and it was half and half really. I've gone off sex altogether now, but my boyfriend hasn't. Sometimes I enjoy it, it depends what mood I'm in, and if she's been playing up. Every time he sees me he thinks I'm going to sleep with him and I don't want to. I'm tired all the time and I'm afraid of getting pregnant again. Even though I am on the Pill. I used to enjoy sex, he can't understand why I don't anymore.

Compared to many of the others, Marie was quite sexually experienced:

I first had sex when I was fourteen. It just happened. Parties. The people I used to hang around with were much older than me anyway, they never knew how old I was. I didn't think much of it the first time. I didn't see what all the fuss was about. It was a quick in-and-out job and I never knew what happened. It's not until you get older that you start experimenting. First couple of times it was very quick. No love or anything. It seemed to please him so I let him get on with it. It got better after that, because then you started meeting blokes who cared about you as well. Then I met my husband and was sure I'd fallen in love with him because he cared so much.

Several had become pregnant on losing their virginity, or very shortly after, and their boyfriends had gone off, leaving them both scarred and scared about having any subsequent sexual relationships. This had happened to Shona, whose boyfriend encouraged her to have the baby, and then left her, with the result that whenever any subsequent boyfriends have tried to get close, she becomes cold and distant, they cannot understand and eventually leave her.

Sexuality is a sensitive subject, laced with complexities. When you are young and still living within the family it is often hard to acknowledge that you are sexually active and need to take some precautions. This is something that many parents also find difficult to accept in their daughters. After the initial shock of discovering their daughter is pregnant, parents have to come to terms with this. As a consequence, mothers especially may become closer to their daughters because they now have the experience of pregnancy and childbirth in common.

But sometimes parents still cannot accept their daughter's sexuality, especially if they return to live in their parents' home. Even though they have a baby, sleeping with their boyfriend may still be regarded with disapproval, unless the baby's father has moved in. Girls themselves may feel very sensitive and embarrassed to be having sex in their parents' house, especially if it was not allowed before. Marie's parents had strong religious views that made her feel very guilty about having sex in their home when she and her husband had to live there for a while: 'We did it on the bedroom floor on the wedding night because I wouldn't use the bed, in case it made a noise. Even though we were married, their religion made me so guilty.'

The difficulties that many girls and boys have in talking to parents about sex and contraception often make it a subject to be mutually avoided.

Learning about sex and birth control

I was told by many teenage mothers that the best thing about having a child so young in life is that you can grow up with your children. The small age gap will bring you closer together, and you will be like friends. This presumably includes talking openly about boyfriends, sex and contraception. This may not turn out to be so easy. Most of the girls I spoke to said they could not talk about these things

13

their mothers, and some of their mothers were no more than seventeen or nineteen years older than themselves. It can be hard to combine parental authority with a friendship that implies equality, and some girls do not even want this. 'How can you tell her things like that – she's your mother.' The teenage years span a period of growing up and finding your own identity. Neither girls nor boys of this age usually want to tell their parents exactly what they are doing, and prefer to preserve some distance, as Denise describes. She had left London without telling anyone, including her mother, that she was pregant. She did not feel very close to her mother, although they had been through some rough times together:

> There's a gap between you because you're always your parents' child. You can't accept them as adults like you and they can't accept you as adults like them. Parents aren't people, they're your parents. And you're their children, you're not people to them. This makes some subjects taboo. You expect your parents to be super-human, and they expect you to be kids forever. You want your parents to come to you first and they want you to come to see them. It's all a bit confusing from both sides.

It is tempting to push the blame, as some young mothers do, on their own mothers for not telling them about sex and contraception. This is not always a fair criticism, as they themselves may have been extremely resistant to being told anything. What would be helpful perhaps is to have a close relationship with a mother-type figure who is not your mother. Someone who could be trusted with confidences, give advice, and yet not be constrained and influenced by being your parent. Relationships like this sometimes do exist, with young aunts or friend's mothers, for instance, and sometimes elder sisters or brothers. But for most girls, if you can't talk to your parents, or your friends, that's it.

14

If talking about boyfriends or sex to your parents has been difficult, asking for contraception may seem impossible. It is a clear admission that you are sexually active, and parents may find this hard to deal with. They may respond in quite contradictory ways, like Bridget's parents. She was thirteen when she started sleeping with her boyfriend:

> When I was younger they used to say if I ever did want to go to bed with somebody to ask to go on the Pill. But after they found out I was sleeping with my boyfriend, my mum said she wasn't going to put me on the Pill because it was the easiest way out. I suppose she meant if she put me on the Pill she was letting me sleep around.

Marie wanted to go on the Pill when she was fifteen:

> I asked Mum if I could go on the Pill. She said, 'I don't know, ask your father.' So I asked Dad, it took me ages, and he said, 'What do you want to go on the Pill for?' I said, 'In case anything happens.' He said, 'Are you having sex?' I couldn't say 'Yes', so I said 'No'. He said, 'Well then, you don't need to go on the Pill.'

Some girls don't even want to ask in case their parents get angry and ban them from seeing their boyfriends. There are mothers and daughters who can talk freely about sex, and mothers who send or accompany their daughter to the doctor to get the Pill, as Tracy's mother had, but they tend to be the exception. Yet studies show that if parents are open about sex with their children and accept their potential sexuality, their daughters are more likely to use contraception. If girls discuss birth control with their mothers, they are more knowledgeable and take more control over this area of their lives. This assumes that girls themselves want to do this, unlike Kate whose response to being given contraceptive pills by her mother was to put them down the toilet.

One study of how teenagers learn about sex and contraception found that for both girls and boys, friends were the most frequent first source of information.[4] Of those whose initial source was parents, most were girls, and more middle-class parents were cited as a first source of information than working-class parents. Working-class children in general were less likely to first learn about sex from parents, and it is less likely that they have positive relationships with their teachers. Although the school is also an important source, it is not always a particularly satisfactory or effective one.

Recent surveys[5] have suggested that parents want their children to learn about these things at school, and from quite an early age. Although some sex education programmes have been introduced into schools, the nature of these has largely depended on the attitudes of the local authority, the individual head teacher, and the teachers assigned to the subject. Their impact and success are also partly determined by the subject area sex education is included under, how it is presented, whether there is any discussion, and whether outside speakers are used, as well as girls' and boys' own willingness to participate. Also whether it includes contraception and abortion, and personal relationships, as well as the 'facts of life'.

But even the most comprehensive programmes may not bridge the gap between information and behaviour. Knowing about methods of preventing pregnancy does not make you go to the doctor or the clinic and ask for them. And a demonstration of the variety of birth control methods available, if not done sensitively, can end up being as unappealing as the contents of a doorstep brush salesman's suitcase. Folasade's recollection of being told about contraception at school was in biology O-level:

There was just this square packet and this rubber thing

shaped like an oval, and a row of yellow pills. That was as far as it went. The cap they showed us was for an elephant, a massive thing. You couldn't get it into perspective at all. The time I was supposed to be going through this a lot of schools were getting a bit of stick because a lot of parents didn't like it. I think we saw a film of the birth of a baby and that was it, sex education in a nutshell. I said once to my biology teacher, 'Why are so many girls getting pregnant?' and she said, 'Didn't you listen in lesson?' I said, 'You didn't tell me anything. Did you tell me where the family planning clinics were, what they do, what age you can get the Pill? Did you tell me how to go about it? You have to search through for yourself. It's either you get pregnant, your friend tells you about contraception, or your mother, apart from that, tough. Sex education – if they're not going to tell you how to and where to, it's pointless. Everyone knows how to sleep with a bloke, or they soon find out, but when do you hear about family planning?

For young women and men to want to use contraception, it has to feel relevant to their lives – something they can actually envisage themselves using. Maybe it would help to bring in people from outside, not just in the form of professionals, such as from family planning clinics, but also people like themselves talking about their own experiences of birth control, pregnancy and motherhood. This is not so easy of course, because some schools take a negative view of pregnant schoolgirls and school-age mothers, and also girls themselves may be extremely loathe to set foot in any school again. They often feel vulnerable, afraid of people's stares, and understandably nervous about discussing such personal and private experiences in this situation. And yet friends and acquaintences of a similar age and background are often those whose views have the most impact.[6] Sara, for instance, personally persuaded two of her pregnant friends to attend the antenatal classes for pregnant teenagers that she went to more effectively than any advertising campaign.

The government has decided to take power over sex education out of the hands of local authorities and give it to school governors and parents. Up to now, the scope and style of any programme depends on the attitudes of the local authority and the individual school. If parents and governors are now to be involved, this may make sex education even more complicated as teachers try to accommodate a variety of differing moral views on what should be taught. As we have seen, parents are not the best communicators of sex education. Meanwhile, girls continue to get unintentionally pregnant.

Parents generally worry less about the sexual behaviour of their sons, and teaching boys about sex and contraception is sometimes considered less crucial than it is for girls. But it takes two to get pregnant, and it is just as important to educate boys about contraception. Few men go to birth control clinics, although the Brook Advisory Clinics have reported a slight increase, and contraception is certainly not a salient feature in men's magazines, where sex never seems to bring such consequences as birth and fatherhood. The Pill has probably been even more liberating for men than it has for women, as men have to worry even less about contraception than they did before. Yet if they become fathers and stay with their partners, this affects them too, and for the rest of their lives.

Using contraception

I think I avoided the issue on purpose. I think that secretly I wanted to get pregnant, although I tried to kid myself I didn't.   (Diane, pregnant at eighteen)

I thought it would never happen to me. I thought my boyfriend would make sure that he knew what he was doing, 'cos at that time I didn't know what I was letting myself in for and also because he was nineteen I said to myself that he was more responsible. (Bridget, pregnant at thirteen)

It did go through my mind a few times, but at the time it doesn't seem that important. (Jenny, pregnant at seventeen)

I was bound to get pregnant, but after the first few times, when I was really scared I thought 'I'll be lucky.'
(Denise, pregnant at sixteen)

The main problem with contraception is that many young women and men know about it, but they don't use it. This gap between learning and behaviour is one through which many fall pregnant.

Lots of young couples do not use contraception on their first time, and many do not use it at all.[7] Although only one in five of the mothers in this book had positively wanted to have a baby, and a few didn't mind, the rest had no particular wish to get pregnant and were rather shocked to discover that they were. Nevertheless, four out of five of them were not using any form of birth control. Of those that were, one was using a sheath, and the others were on the Pill. Since having their babies, most were using contraception, generally in the form of the Pill.

Few had discussed contraception with their boyfriends. Ever since the Pill took over from the sheath in availability and popularity, the onus of responsibility has fallen even more heavily on women. Many men simply assume that women are on the Pill and don't even bother to ask. On the first few dates or longer, some young couples are too embarrassed to talk about it, let alone go and do anything about it, and girls don't want to be seen as anticipating sex and run the risk of being labelled as slags. Alan thought men could be more responsible:

> Men should be more careful. I think they should find out if the girl's on the Pill or not. But for some people it's not easy to discuss it. The times I've had to go in and get Durex for somebody else, because they haven't the nerve. Nine times out of ten it's a female behind the counter. It even embarrasses me, but I do it. I know now that you can get Durex free from family planning clinics, but not many people know that. But then how many fellas will go into a family planning clinic? I don't know what it's like for a girl, but it's not easy for a fella to get hold of contraception. I think a lot of fellas think it's her responsibility. It's her that gets unstuck if she doesn't use it. But I think if Durex were free and readily available, fellas would be more responsible.

Since the advent of the Pill, the condom or sheath (Durex) has fallen in popularity. However, with the current serious concern at the spread of the disease AIDS (Acquired Immune Deficiency Syndrome), people are reconsidering its value, not only as a form of contraception, but as protection against the AIDS virus. This attacks the body's immune system, which is its defence against infection, and at present there is no known cure. The virus is most effectively passed on through blood or semen, and has to enter the bloodstream to become established. Therefore it can be contracted by having sexual intercourse with an infected individual. If you are contemplating having sex with someone who you have not known for very long, and do not know much about, you are strongly advised to use a condom during intercourse. This also protects you against other sexually transmitted diseases such as gonorrhoea and herpes, and vaginal infections like thrush.

Young men may be more concerned with doing it right to start with, rather than with using contraception. Then when it 'just happens', spontaneously and romantically, they and their girlfriends hope they don't get pregnant, or they don't think about it at all. And one study looking at the experiences of black teenage mothers found that although they had begun using contraceptives as much as white girls, some had been persuaded by their boyfriends to stop using them.[8] This was linked to ideas of motherhood as confirming both male virility, and adult femininity.

Ironically, at the start of a relationship it may not seem relevant to use anything as nothing may happen, so it may not seem worth all that trouble to get the Pill. And the more unstable a relationship is, the less likely it is that contraception will be used. Yet one study showed that about one in five of all premarital pregnancies occur in the first month of a sexual relationship, and half within the first six months. Several of the young mothers here, for instance, had got pregnant almost straightway, two from their first and only sexual experience.

If a relationship is clearly becoming either more established, or girls (and boys) are moving on to other sexual relationships, it seems logical to take precautions. But although many have been told about birth control by friends or parents, and may have had this information included in lessons at school, relatively few do anything about it. 'Why didn't you use anything?' is a familiar question, and there are various explanations – getting pregnant may have an unreal quality about it, something which younger teenagers in particular may feel, and even if they know the risks they assume that they'll be lucky. Some have a fatalistic approach that if it happens, it happens. There are also those old myths still around about when you don't get pregnant – like if it's your first time, or if you have sex infrequently, or if you do it standing up.

An important step towards seeking contraception is to acknowledge to yourself that you are a sexually active person. This can be difficult if part of you thinks it is wrong and you shouldn't really be doing it. Getting contraception then seems like a public and official recognition of having sex and may be a psychological barrier that some girls may be reluctant to cross. At Folasade's school, asking someone if she was on the Pill was the way of asking her if she was sleeping with her boyfriend or not. Girls who are very aware of parental disapproval may not feel able to take this step and also not want to run the risk of parents somehow finding out that they had gone to the doctor or the clinic. Some are also unaware or confused about where to obtain birth control and what this involves. One girl told me she had even thought family planning clinics were where a woman went with her husband and children to plan their future together.

Some young women are too embarrassed to ask their doctors and afraid of being refused, especially if they are under age. The Victoria Gillick campaign to deny contraceptive advice to girls under sixteen without their parents' consent did a great deal of harm in this respect. Even though her aim was eventually defeated, it led to a lot of confusion amongst teenagers which still persists. Refusing to give contraception to young girls is not going to stop sexual activity; all it means is that more run the risk of pregnancy, which can be far more dangerous. Take Denise, for instance, who had told her boyfriend she was on the Pill when she wasn't:

When we started having sex I was fifteen and scared that if I went on the Pill the doctor would tell my mum. I promised myself I would go on the Pill as soon as I was sixteen. I did make an appointment at the local family planning clinic. I was going to go down with my mate. Then she couldn't go so I didn't go on my own. When

I finally went for the (pregnancy) test, I thought, this is it, this is the point where I go on the Pill. But of course it was too late.

Although many doctors are sympathetic, prescribing contraception is left to their discretion and so there are a few who refuse to give it, with or without parental consent. At fifteen, Melanie went with her mother's permission to her doctor to ask for the Pill, but this was refused. The result is her five-month-old daughter.

Another result of the ease and availability of the Pill is an assumption that this is more or less the only method of birth control. It is the Pill or nothing. Young men and women tend to dislike the other more mechanical methods, such as using a sheath, diaphragm or cap, which although quite effective, are seen as too planned as well as being comparatively messy. And many women don't like the idea of having a coil fitted inside them. So if a girl does not feel able to go and ask for the Pill, or if she is reluctant to use it because she sees it as a health risk, the alternative may be to use nothing. But the Pill is not suitable for some girls, who have a lot of problems and side effects using it. Claire and Nickie were both in the process of changing pills when they fell pregnant.

Given the information about birth control, whether or not young women go in search of contraception crucially depends on their motivation to do so. This in turn depends on the relevance it has, how important it is to them not to get pregnant, and how easy emotionally and practically it is to go somewhere and ask for it. Girls (and boys) need to know how to approach people about contraception and feel confident enough to do it. Having got it, it also needs continued motivation and commitment, especially in the case of the Pill which has to be taken every day without fail, otherwise it is not totally effective.

Boyfriends

The first person to hear about a pregnancy is often the boyfriend involved, assuming he is still around. Some relationships have already split up before girls realise that their periods have stopped or they feel a bit sick, and they discover they are well and truly pregnant. In such cases, telllng the baby's father often produces a quick denial of paternity or support. Sometimes both partners have started new relationships in the intervening time. Perhaps the relationship is still continuing, but the boyfriend does not want to know about pregnancy. His reaction is 'get rid of it!' Jenny's boyfriend left her with that attitude, and this made her even more determined to keep her baby.

Sometimes boyfriends may go though a radical change of heart in the middle of the pregnancy. Their reaction turns from pleasure to indifference or hostility as they realise what impending fatherhood actually involves. This can be very upsetting, especially if their promises of love and support were an important factor in girls wanting to continue their pregnancies. Wendy's boyfriend was pleased with the idea of being a father at first but he could never really come to terms with the reality of it, nor his responsibilities. He went out with other girls, spent Wendy's money, and knocked her about.

The age of consent for a girl to have sexual intercourse is sixteen, and therefore any male over fourteen having sex with a girl under sixteen has actually committed an illegal act. When Cathy got pregnant at fourteen by the lodger who until recently had lived in her family's home, her parents decided to take him to court. They were extremely angry, feeling that he had taken advantage of her age and vulnerability, and he also had several other children with women in the same area. Parents take this course of action relatively rarely, however, because it can clearly be a very

24

traumatic experience for both the girl and their family, as Cathy had found:

> They dragged me to the Police Station where I had to make a detailed statement of everything that had happened the first time intercourse took place. And I had to say this in front of my mother who had to be present, which was even more degrading. I felt quite dirty having to tell all these intimate details to total strangers and most of all my mother, who I had to live with and would always know everything, as they are not the sort of things you discuss with your parents.
>
> At first they asked me if I wanted my mum to go out but I said No, but when they started asking me all those sorts of questions they asked me again and I said Yes. So my mum went out but then she still had to read it all because I was under-age and she had to be there. They had made an exception, but she still had to come in and read it. It made me feel horrible.

As Cathy was several months pregnant by this time, she subsequently had her daughter, who is now two years old. She has not been out with anyone else since this happened, and is very cautious about having any other relationships.

Many prospective fathers are, however, overjoyed at the prospect of parenthood, and do stay around to give love and support to their partners. In cases where marriage has been discussed, pregnancy is not unwelcome, and may even have been anticipated, as it had been for Claire, who married her husband when she was five months pregnant. Folasade and her boyfriend had both been pleased when she got pregnant; they were still together after three years and hoping to build a stable future for themselves. Lindsey and Pete had started talking about having a baby when she was fourteen, and did so the following year:

Pete and me had been together for eleven months and loved each other more than words could say. When we first found out, our relationship became a bit rocky and when I was three months pregnant, Pete walked out on me. But he came back three days later crying his eyes out and begging me to forgive him, he looked like a helpless puppy. After that we became disinterested in each other and I only had three weeks to the deadline, a last-minute decision to make, but I suppose I'm one of the lucky ones because my parents were behind me all the way.

But Pete did stay around, and they live together in her parents' house with their nine-month-old baby. He reflects back on how he felt:

I didn't know what to do. A lot of my mates said if they were going out with someone and they got pregnant they would run. I told them they didn't know what it was like. When it happens to you it's totally different. It changes you. I've got a responsibility now. That's how I look at it. I've got something out of life now. It doesn't bother me. If anyone takes the mickey I turn round and say 'I've got a daughter.' That's all that matters. It did get a bit rocky after she became pregnant. I just sat down and sorted it out. I was all right after that. Just getting over the shock. Being single all the time, and suddenly landed, if you know what I mean.

What happens to those who are already going out with another boyfriend when they discover they are pregnant? How is he going to take this news? In Bridget's case, her subsequent boyfriend stayed around for a year or so until she and her family moved house. He kept her company and gave her support when she was pregnant and didn't like to go out. Alan met Lesley when she was already pregnant as a result of a brief incident at a party that she can barely remember. They live together and as far as he is concerned, he will treat her daughter as his own.

For teenage mothers on their own, the prospect of meeting and going out with boys may not be easy. Some have become extremely wary of men through their experiences, and feel suspicious and distrustful. They are sometimes loathe to tell men that they have a baby for fear of being rebuffed or being seen as easy, like Shona, now twenty with a daughter of two:

> Now I feel it is very hurtful when you have a boyfriend and when he finds out he doesn't want to know in case the child calls him Daddy. I begin to really hate men and don't want to get close to them in case I get hurt again. I don't understand them and think that I'm never going to meet anybody nice that will accept me as a single parent. They seem to think because you have a child you're an easy catch to bed and breakfast.

Some feel too vulnerable to cope with having boyfriends at all, at least not for some time, and almost all are determined that any man who shows an interest in them will have to accept and love their child too.

Another option open to any single mother is to sue the baby's father for child maintenance. This may be inappropriate if he is very young, or long since gone, but it can be worthwhile. Bringing up a child is hard work and expensive on your own. Quite a lot of young girls, however, choose not to sue for child maintenance. They often feel that because the relationship has finished, maybe on a sour note, or the father has shown little interest in his child, they don't want any more to do with him. Receiving maintenance payments would perpetuate this link and also gives him unwelcome paternity rights. And if a mother is on social security, as many are, his payments get included in this total amount, so it means no extra money in the hand.

Something that concerned several mothers I talked to who were on their own, was what to tell their children about their real father when they are old enough to know. Sometimes he may live nearby, although there may be no contact whatsoever. Some too were worried, like other single mothers, that their baby had no immediate father figure around.

Certainly not all boyfriends of teenage mothers are teenagers themselves, although a significant number of them are quite young. The ages of those involved with the mothers talking here ranged between sixteen and thirty-five when their babies were born, but the majority were aged between seventeen and twenty-two. They didn't all desert their girlfriends when they became pregnant, some have remained to provide crucial emotional and practical support. However, about two-thirds of the mothers in this book are no longer with their baby's father. Either he left when he discovered the pregnancy, or he had already gone, or the relationship had broken up in the first year or two after having the baby, when he had been unwilling or unable to settle down and take the responsibility. For most of these young mothers, their parents have proved to be a more sustaining source of support than their baby's father. Those with older boyfriends seemed to fare better; for instance, two with partners in their thirties were much more economically and socially secure. Other boyfriends, like Alan, who describes living with Lesley and her baby daughter in the following pages, may be more supportive than the baby's own father. Also illustrating this chapter, Charlene and Wendy describe their experiences with boyfriends, pregnancy and motherhood.

FOLASADE

Folasade is an eighteen-year-old whose daughter, Natalie, is almost three years old. She is redoing her A-levels in chemistry, physics and biology in the sixth form of a London girls' school. She has applied to do a nursing degree. She and her daughter live most of the week with her mother, who works as a night nurse, and her sister and brother. They spend the remaining part at her West Indian boyfriend's home. Folasade's parents come from Nigeria, where her father returned when she was seven years old.

She met Michael, her boyfriend, when she was fourteen and he was nineteen. A year later, when she was working for her O-levels, she became pregnant. She had miscalculated her dates, so when she went into labour she thought she was only five months pregnant and having a miscarriage. As she had told no one except her boyfriend that she was pregnant, it came as a shock to her family. (The story of Natalie's birth is related in Chapter 4.)

Going back to school was never a problem. The school easily agreed to take her back, her friends were pleased to see her, and her daughter goes to day nursery on the days when she has to be in school. Folasade has many plans for the future. She and her boyfriend will get married, study for their careers, get a place to live, and she wants several more children. Her dream is to be the director of a children's hospital; her boyfriend will own his own garage and she hopes that they'll live happily ever after.

'When I discovered I was pregnant, Michael was more worried for me and what would happen at school and with my mum than anything else. About four months before, a friend of mine got pregnant and she had to have an abortion, and I was quite upset about that. So I said, if I got pregnant what would you want me to do?

And he said, he supposed that an abortion would be the sensible thing, but he would like to have kept the child. We didn't dwell on it that long. So when I was actually pregnant, although it would be fairer on me and the baby and everybody concerned if I did have an abortion, he made me know that he didn't really want me to have one. He would like to have the baby. I wasn't going to have an abortion anyway, I was going to keep my baby. I've got very strange ideals, and one of the things I've got a very definite mind on is abortion. I can understand the reason for other people having them, but I can't really see myself having it. So I said, "That's good."

There were smiles all round, we were smiling secretly at each other. It was nice, because he sort of stood by me. He was very reassuring. I'm quite an independent person, but I was quite insecure, I needed someone to say this is good, this is bad, and because he was doing that it gave me the determination I needed. It was nice. I wasn't sitting at home crying into my pillow. It was there a bit because I was hiding something from my mother. I told my boyfriend but I couldn't tell my mum. I didn't feel I could tell her on my own. He felt that I should tell her on my own. Mum had only met him once and that was it. It was very secret. So, it was like a relief that I could talk to him about being pregnant. But I still wanted to tell my Mum. It was the first thing I'd ever kept from her. Going back out with Michael, and being pregnant, and still she doesn't know. It was horrid to do, it was very unfortunate, because every time, like, when we were alone together, I'd say it in my head – I'm pregnant, I'm pregnant – but my mum really flares up, she goes crazy. So I thought, I'll tell her after my exams. And what happened was, the exam finished Friday, and I had the baby on Sunday. I thought I had ages and ages. But I didn't. So I never actually told her.

I thought at first she had taken it well, and then she went

crazy. She exploded at me in the hospital. I felt betrayed.
Why do it now, why didn't she do it in the first place. I was
comfortable, I had just accepted things how they were. But
we've got a very close-knit family, in that if two people
aren't getting on, everybody in the family will make them
be friends. So when things go wrong, they're always there.
So everything was all right after a little while. And after a
few months, my mum and Michael managed to sort out
their differences. So from then on it was just, get on with it.
I think at first she blamed Michael, the first few days. Then
it was "You're a naughty child" sort of thing, and it all fell on
to me. But now it's like that part never happened, we're
just one big happy family.

I didn't feel I was able to tell her I was pregnant right
from the start. Some girls have the relationship with their
mothers that if anything happens they can tell their
mother. But in our house, everything is very very
secretive. You tell your sister, but you don't tell your
mother. You hear about these girls going with their parents
to the family planning clinic, my mum would never do that.
My mum never warned me about getting pregnant
because she thought I was a good girl. My sister was the
person who'd been the trouble, she had had boyfriends in
infant school, I was the girl who always beat up the boys in
infant school! I was totally uninterested in boys, apart from
playing football with them. Up to about the age of fourteen.
All the warning had been thrown at her, and I wasn't
interested in blokes, so I didn't need it. My mum's attitude
was "You can have boyfriends, but don't have boyfriends".
I asked her, "Would you mind if I have a boyfriend?" and
she said "It depends" and I said "What if I said somebody
wanted to take me to the pictures?" and it was, "If a boy
wants to take you to the pictures, he's only after one thing.
He gives you an ice cream and you give him a kiss", that
sort of thing. That was the last thing she ever said about

blokes. But I still went out with Michael.

At first when I started sleeping with Michael, I thought, there's no reason to say no. Apart from my age. So I did. But it was very much for him. I thought, well this is what everybody does, this is what you're supposed to do. I didn't realise that I could enjoy it for myself, not just for him. I didn't enjoy it when it happened the first time. I just slept with him. There were times when I tried to tell him before that I was just sleeping with him because he wanted to sleep with me, but he's a person who can get easily upset, and I didn't want to hurt him. In our sexual relationship he's been very good. Now, perhaps because I've had a baby, friends talk to me about sex, or about their relationships with their boyfriends, where before they wouldn't. I can accept it now. But before it was, no, don't talk to me about it. I didn't want to know. And even though I'd had the baby, I was still very naive. I didn't use any contraception. I was so stupid. Up till the age of, about sixteen, after my birthday, the baby would have been a few weeks old, I thought well, if you're under sixteen, don't think about the Pill, they're not going to give it to you. I never actually spoke to anybody about boyfriends, contraceptives, intercourse, whatever, I just sort of picked little things up, I thought if you were under sixteen either your parents came with you or you don't get anything. I thought there was no way my mum was going to hold my hand down the clinic. Now I know that she probably would have done. She wouldn't have liked me sleeping with him, but if you're going to sleep with him, you get contraceptives. So I thought, sixteenth birthday. Then by my sixteenth birthday, I'd already had the baby.

When I was in the hospital after I'd had Baby, a bloke came round with the different contraceptives, saying which one are you going to use. My mum wanted me to say, well I don't need any, I won't be sleeping with him.

And I knew for a little while that would be true. But for the long term, for me to let her carry on thinking that way would be stupid, I'd be starting another one all over again. So I said "I'll take something just in case, if you don't mind, Mother." It was a chance to start afresh. She was there with me and she knew these people were asking me. It would have been stupid to say I wasn't going to sleep with him, because I knew I would. And the Pill was the easiest way. Even the Pill, I'm very bad with. I have one month when I take it on the dot, every day, I then forget, and I think, oh God I'm pregnant. I'm getting better with it. I still don't like the idea of having to take it, but it's just something you've got to do. If you don't want a baby, take the Pill. I knew I could get pregnant when I was sleeping with Michael before. At the time we were doing withdrawal, which is pointless, but we were doing something. I used to say, oh God, what if I get pregnant. It was something that was more or less always on my mind. But it didn't stop me sleeping with him. He was constantly saying, when am I going to get the Pill. And this particular time I said, well maybe we should use Durex. And then it was who was going to buy them. You can buy them, no you buy them. In the end he got them. I think we tried to use it once, and it was like a comedy show, it was crazy. I've still got the packet at home, to remember the day by. But I think it was, "it hasn't happened so far, so why should it?"

At school there's always the two or three girls in the class that you know are sleeping with guys, and they had no qualms about it. But it's like – in the third year it's "have you got your periods?" and then the fourth year "have you slept with your boyfriend?" But then when I had Baby, and came back, everybody was telling me, this girl's got pregnant, that girl's had an abortion, this girl's done this, this girl's done that. I thought I was the bad bad girl, but everybody else was doing exactly the same. When you come back, because you've had a baby, they feel free to talk to you. Obviously you've slept with a bloke if you've got a baby. It's a bit like being a member of a club. It's crazy. And maybe because I went to an all girls' school, it's not so obvious, you don't see girls and boys walking hand in hand in the playground. I think it wasn't seen as good or bad to sleep with your boyfriend. It's like, girls who had on that side, and girls who hadn't on that side, – can I join, kind of thing. It was just something you had or hadn't done. But there was this thing about virgins, in class. It wasn't bad, it was – well, I know something you don't know but you'll find out. I wasn't considered a slag. If girls are considered slags, they are considered slags from before, because they had slept with guys when they were young, and they had this, that and the other guy. Only true slags are slags. If you slept with a boy and he was your boyfriend, it didn't really matter.

I couldn't believe how many people had had abortions when I went back to school. I think it's crazy. Not for the fact that, Oh God, abortions are bad, how come so many people have had them? It's just that to have an abortion you have to be pregnant, so all these people have got pregnant. It's amazing. It's not such a magnificent thing that I've got pregnant, it's just I'm the only one that's kept it. Before it was, why me, nobody else gets pregnant. But then I found out lots of people have got pregnant, they just had abortions. They're usually on the Pill before they have abortions. They're just a bit careless. There's only one girl of my age that I've known who's on the cap. But everybody else is on the Pill. You say, "Are you on the Pill?" "Yes, I'm on the Pill." That's the way you find out if they've slept with somebody, ask them if they're on the Pill.

When mum first met Michael she didn't mind that he's West Indian and not Nigerian. But when Baby came she thought if it was a Nigerian boy it would have been so easy.

34

But that's just because of the way she knows Nigerian boys are brought up at home. Little does she know that Nigerian boys here aren't the same. We've got this thing about respect, anyone one second older than you, you respect them. Your father, your mother, you know. West Indians have it, but not to the same degree. She had this thing that if it had been a Nigerian boy, the mother would be here saying "I'm sorry my son has got your daughter pregnant." They'd be talking for days on end. So when she was going on about Nigerian boys, I said, "So what, if I went out with this guy, you'd be lucky if he stayed with me." I said, "Michael's come, Michael's still here and he doesn't have to be here." So from that angle she was sort of grateful that anybody was there. I suppose inside though she would rather it was a Nigerian boy. Michael still lives with his mum and I live with my mum, but if I sleep up my house, he sleeps up my house. If I sleep at his house, he sleeps there. We're always together. We're planning to get a flat. We've already bought most of the stuff to put in the flat, half at my house and half at his house. Marriage, or engagement is on the cards for next February. It was something that was already planned before I got pregnant. I'm not the sort who can go out with someone unless my feelings were so deep that I can imagine spending my life with them, and having a child. And the same thing with Michael. Even though he was so much older, I was his first girlfriend, he was my first boyfriend.'

WENDY

Wendy is eighteen and lives with her twenty-month-old daughter Lucy, and two white mice in the ground floor flat of a high-rise council block on a bleak council estate. She was sixteen, working as a sewing machinist and engaged to her boyfriend Keith when she became pregnant. They had

often fantasised about how nice it would be to have a baby.
Her mother had brought her up in the strict religion of the
Mormon church, which made her very guilty about having
sex. She and Keith moved into a cold, damp flat together
when she was pregnant, from which they were moved into
a hotel before ending up in her present home, on the out-
skirts of a sprawling town.

Although he was initially delighted to be a father, Keith
was totally unable to cope with the responsibility and came
and went in their relationship as he pleased, giving little
help or support. Wendy had more idea of what to expect,
she had helped to look after her little brothers at home, but
it was still hard work having a baby of her own. She had
always been quite dependent on Keith, which was why he
got away with such a lot, but eventually she has grown
more confident, and believes that she can now make it on
her own.

'I knew almost straightaway that I was pregnant. I was
due on Keith's seventeenth birthday. It's funny, Lucy
wasn't exactly planned, I think I thought I would never get
pregnant. Keith and I had got engaged four months before
and we said if I did get pregnant we would get married but
we never did. Every month when I came on we would say,
never mind, next time. Then it came to March and I didn't
come on. Even though I knew I was pregnant, I kept
thinking, no, I can't be. Something changed in me and I
suddenly felt very scared, but Keith said don't worry about
a thing, I'll take care of you.

I hadn't gone on the Pill because I didn't want to admit
that I was doing something wrong, because mum had
always brought me up that it was wrong before marriage.
Also my auntie went on the Pill and she became infertile.
But then I started to think, well at this rate I am going to get
pregnant, so I decided to go on the Pill, and that was the

month I fell for Lucy. Also Keith thought he couldn't have any children because he'd been out with a girl for a year before I started going out with him and they didn't take any precautions and she never got pregnant.

Mum told me the facts of life when I was twelve. I was so shocked, it just didn't register. She had to tell me three times before it sunk in. I kept saying, "How do you do it again?" But I had a very strict Mormon church upbringing and it was not exactly a taboo subject, but it was just taken for granted that you didn't do that until you got married. So there was no need to talk about these sort of things. Mum told me about the various forms of contraception but apart from that we didn't really talk about it.

I'd been out with other boys other than Keith but they never touched me. With Keith, I fell head over heels in love with him from the first time we met, and I'd only been going out with him two weeks and he asked me to get engaged. I was very much in love. And it just happened. I cried my eyes out afterwards though. I don't know why. That I'd actually done it I suppose. He said, "You all right? What's the matter?" I can't say that I did honestly enjoy it at first. I had more guilt feelings than anything else. Like I'd betrayed my mum. I was sort of torn between my mum and Keith then. And I lost all my urge to go to church, because I felt I was doing wrong, so I didn't go, and then I didn't have the strong principles anymore.

Just before I got pregnant, Keith had started hitting me. We used to have arguments, mainly over my going to church. He used to say that I loved God more than I loved him. He is a very jealous person. He had told me that he didn't want to go out with me anymore. I cried my eyes out, I felt so lost and lonely, he couldn't do this to me, not after all he'd said. Anyway it ended up in a fight and he started pushing me around and went to punch me in the stomach but I managed to stop him. Then he ran

out and left me crying on the kitchen floor. I went
into the sitting room and there I was, tear-stained face
and red marks when Keith's mother came in. "What on
earth has happened to you?" she said. I just blurted out,
"I think I am pregnant and Keith doesn't want me
anymore." When she'd calmed down she asked me if I'd
been to the doctors, and we made arrangements for her to
take me down.

When we told my mum, she started to make plans for
me and Keith to get married. I was always very close to her.
I wasn't very close to my dad at all. At one stage I thought
he used to pick on me. When I told my mum I was
pregnant she phoned my dad up. As he was doing night
work I didn't see him until Saturday when we had a good
heart-to-heart talk, it was really nice. I'd never felt he
cared for me but at last we sat and talked. He said, "I've
talked to Mum about it and if you don't want to get married
then no one is going to force you to. If you want to stay here
with the baby you can or if you want to go with Keith that's
okay with me." After that things with my dad were so
much better.

I was such a goody-goody at school it was unbelievable
that I was pregnant. Everyone was totally shocked. I was
the last person anyone thought would get pregnant. We'd
often talked about it and I'd always said, No, I would never
do anything like that unitl I got married. Very sure of
myself then. Things change!

Keith was over the moon at first at the prospects of being
a father, but that all changed. It hit home, what it involved.
He said he was scared about all the girls he'd miss going
out with, stuck with one girl. So when I was pregnant
he went out with somebody else. So we finished. Then we
got back together again and I was living with him at his
mum's house.

I felt special when I was pregnant and carrying this little

person inside me. But it started to make me feel scared that it was something I was going to have to bring up for the rest of my life. It's different having a child of your own to bringing up your brothers.

When I was seven months pregnant we decided to get a flat of our own. It was strange at first because I was used to Mum cooking dinners. Keith was working then. He was a presser, although he had a number of jobs. I used to lie down and have a sleep because I got very tired towards the end with the baby. He used to come back and say, "Where's my dinner?" and start moaning at me. His mum spoilt him a lot, he was the youngest, and was used to having everything done for him. He used to say, "Mum does it like this." He stayed in the flat until Lucy was about two months old then he left again. He went home for about two weeks and then came back again. Keith was a right proud Dad. When we used to go to town he used to get her out and carry her. I wasn't allowed to push the pushchair. But once we got home that was it. All back on me. He used to help out now and again, but only when he felt like it.

The flat was an absolute dump. It was the attic part of an old house. It was in a terrible state when we moved in but we cleaned it up and made it quite homely. But finally the Social moved us out of there because we had no hot water. We had to go downstairs to the toilet, and in the winter the water used to freeze up. The electric bill used to be so high because we had the electric fire on all the time and we used to leave the oven on as well. Frozen breath came out of your mouth otherwise. So they moved us out into a hotel. Keith stayed with us there for about three weeks. Then he accused me of going off with everyone there, which was totally untrue. Then he hit me, so nobody spoke to him, and he moved out. Me and Lucy stayed there another five or six months on our own. I didn't like living in the hotel at first. It was quite a way from the area I'd been brought up in, but I got to like it and make friends, and I got more independent. But it was horrible being in one tiny room. Just the beds, wash basin, little cupboard. You couldn't swing a cat in there. Once Lucy was in the cot you could just squeeze in the door. Keith didn't give any financial support because he wasn't working then.

Then the social worker got us this flat and Keith moved in with us, and he stayed until just before Christmas, and we've been on our own ever since. When we moved in here, he took out a loan because he's in a band and wanted a new guitar, but we couldn't afford the payments on Social. I had to go out to work. He tried to get a job but he couldn't. I worked as a dress machinist. I only worked there for about two months, I was so tired I was like a zombie. I was paying for bills, food and everything from my wages. I used to get home absolutely exhausted from work and he was sitting there and he'd say, "What's for dinner then?" He looked after Lucy during the day while I was at work, but I found out afterwards that he used to leave her a lot with my friends upstairs. He'd take her up and she had only her vest on and her socks, and this was getting winter time, so I thought I can't have that.

At first I didn't take any notice that he wasn't helping me. I used to just let him get away with it. But when we moved in here, because I'd been away from him for five months and I'd learned to cope for myself, I started standing up for myself and he didn't like it. He said I'd changed. I wasn't depending on him anymore. I said what do you expect?

I hate being on the Social. They give you just enough money to survive. I'd like to get nice things but I can't. The social worker organised some furniture for us. This old fella had died and she took us there to choose what we wanted which was horrible. They gave me a cheque for some stuff, but Keith just wanted to spend it and didn't really think about what he was buying. The cheques were in his name so I didn't really have a lot of say in it. He bought some clothes and records. I wasn't too pleased about that. I wanted to get some nice curtains.

The worse thing is being on my own. During the days I go and see my friends, most of the people who were at the hotel at the same time as I was have been moved up here. But it's the night times, sitting here when Lucy's in bed. I think, what can I do now? But I don't mind living here, it's all right. Even though I'm not one to go out, some days you wish you didn't have someone dependent on you and could just go out and about. Even if someone looks after her you wonder, is he all right? You think, what was it like not to have this little thing to care about? I can't even remember just being me. All I remember now is me and Lucy.

I've always wanted children. I want at least four when I do finally settle down and get married. I love kids, but it was never an obsession. At first, with Keith, we were so wrapped up with ourselves. We talked about it and said it would be nice to have a baby. But I don't think Keith was prepared for everything that went with it. I wasn't totally prepared but I knew what it was like. We thought it would be a nice idea.

I have been out with a couple of people, but I can't see myself with anybody else but Keith. Still. It doesn't feel right. A couple of months ago he wanted to come back but I said there's no way he'd come back here without us being married. I'd never live with anybody now until I was married. I've changed over the last couple of years. I'm more independent. I can stand up for myself. Before when Keith left I'd be a total wreck. I love Lucy, but at the time he was more important to me than she was, in one sense. But I'm not dependent anymore, he's not worth it. He still hasn't grown up. He's the same as he ever was. He doesn't want to work. He wants to go out when he wants. Even with all his bills to pay he'd rather go to the pub. So he still can't handle responsibility. He's back home where his mum does all his cooking, washing and ironing for him. He's got it made.

I didn't feel loved before, but now I have somebody that's dependent on me, I have something of my own to love, and she loves me back. I wasn't looking for something to fill my life by having her, she just happened. I think whatever age you have a child, if it's fine for you, then it's all right. But unless you're really sure that you want a baby and all that goes with it, think twice. It's not just something you can dress up and take for walks in the park. There's a lot more to it.

Before I had to feel secure and loved, but now it doesn't bother me. I feel secure in the sense that I'm my own sort of person and I feel loved by Lucy. Obviously that's not the sort of love I would have got from Keith or whoever, it's not secure like there's someone looking after me. There are times when I wish I had someone to look after and who would look after me again, but I am confident now I can do it on my own.'

ALAN

Alan is twenty-two and lives with Lesley, now aged seventeen, and her ten-month-old daughter in a northern coastal town. They have one room and a kitchen in a large house, and share bathroom facilities. Before Lesley met Alan, she had been to a party where she got drunk and ended up sleeping with someone without knowing it. She suspected that she was pregnant when she began seeing Alan, but this was only confirmed when she had to go for a check-up because Alan had a urinal infection. Her father and mother are divorced and she was living with her father, her stepmother, her sister and brother, and a stepsister and stepbrother. She was responsible for a lot of the housework and looked after her younger brothers and sisters. She was arranging to have an abortion when her father found out, and told her if she went through with this, he would no longer consider her to be part of his family. So she decided to have the baby.

She was still at school, and sat her exams when she was four or five months pregnant. She and Alan lived together at her father's house until after she had the baby, an experience that Alan did not enjoy. At seven months pregnant, she started bleeding a lot and was rushed to hospital. The baby was born by Caesarean section and went straight into special care for five-and-a-half weeks. After they had brought her home, she developed a collapsed lung, pneumonia, and later gastroenteritis, which landed her in hospital again. At ten months, she seems fine.

They are both living on social security, although Alan has had various jobs in the past. He has worked in shops, factories and stores, and has trained in engraving and drycleaning, and has worked as a medical assistant. He had wanted Lesley to have an abortion, but because he feels committed to Lesley he is prepared to bring up the baby as if she were his own.

'I knew she was pregnant when we started going out. I knew that I liked Lesley, and that was all that was important. I just went along with her and supported her with whatever she did. Her real mum gave her a lot of support, and so did I. But supporting her doesn't mean hiding what I think. I wanted her to have an abortion because it would have given us more time to get ourselves sorted out and get our life going together before bringing another person into it. But we didn't get that chance.

We'd set on living together, and seeing how it worked out, with or without the baby. But it was a hard decision.

What angered me most was the way her dad went about it and her stepmum, giving her ultimatums. Telling her she'd have to get out and she wasn't part of the family and all that. To me they were ordering her to have the baby, which wasn't fair. They said they'd give a lot of help. But they're not going to be there after five or six years to help. A baby, to me, is a lifelong thing. It's for the rest of our lives really. To me she's my daughter now. We've got to keep her at least until she's sixteen.

We both had thought about having the baby. You see, I'm a very practical person, I think of whether we'll be able to do things. Lesley's more of the heart, if it's set on something she'll do it. When she was thinking about having an abortion nobody told her to have it. I think she wanted the baby but she was going to have the abortion because she realised the possibility of a better life. But I think she was fairly relieved to have the situation taken out of her hands by her parents telling her what to do.

The only way we can do anything now is with help from somebody else. For money and things like that. We can't get a house because we're not working. Even things people take for granted we can't do. It's tied us down a lot. We can't just nip on a coach and go somewhere for the day. It stops you doing things I think couples should do before they start a family. If she'd had the abortion it would have given us time to do that sort of thing.

We lived with her parents for a short while before she had the baby. I didn't like living there. To me it's the unhappiest house I've ever been to. I used to hate sitting there, so in the end I never bothered. The family never really put much pressure on me, they put more pressure on Lesley. If they ever wanted to have a moan about anything I did wrong, like using the bathroom too often, they used to tell Lesley to tell me. I used to go mad. What's wrong with telling me? I'm virtually one of the family now.

If I thought they were doing anything wrong to Lesley I couldn't say anything because she'd get it, I wouldn't get it. So that made me unhappy, and in turn made Lesley unhappy, so it wasn't a very good situation.

We're on social security and we've virtually had to fight for everything we've got. We manage just about. But if they ever cut the money or knock something off, we'd be in deep. If we want to buy anything at the moment we have to borrow the money. Even if I was still working I don't think we'd be able to buy anything outright. Every time we save a bit of money we find something we have to spend it on. With the HP you have to pay it, so we do. We get £93 including the rent. If I get a job now I've got to get one that pays £110 or £120 which isn't all that easy. So it's not worth getting a job because we won't be as well off.

We go out in the day together, we try to go to town once a week, and every Sunday we go to my aunty's house. Lesley goes out about one night a week and I go out occasionally. Although we go out quite a lot, we just go for walks. That's the main problem, if we want to go anywhere, it costs money to get there. I do the difficult cooking, Lesley does things like beans on toast. I do look after the baby a little bit but I don't often change her nappies. I can look after her, but I don't know about every single day. When the baby cries a lot, and Lesley gets angry with her, I tell her to go off for an hour and I'll look after her.

I wouldn't like another baby for another three or four years at least. I don't really like this situation. It's not the real way to bring up a child. And when she starts seeing things she wants, that her mates have got, we might not be able to afford things, because we've sort of been dumped in this situation.

The main thing that upsets me is the fact that she's a bastard. I never found out that I was a bastard until I was eighteen. That hurt me. My father's my dad but they never told me they weren't married. I don't want that handle on the baby at all. I'll be telling her as soon as she can understand. It's upsetting to find you were born out of wedlock. It upsets me. I'd rather Lesley had had an abortion and tried for a kid when we were married. But we've got no intentions of getting married at the moment. The only benefit of getting married now is the Family Income Supplement, that's only £7 a week.

I'm pretty easygoing, no problems. I like Lesley, I think that's all that matters really. You can't alter the past. I know that from experience. Quite a lot had gone wrong in my life. What's done is done. A few years back I got a girl pregnant and I think she was forced to have an abortion, which is opposite to Lesley. Lesley was forced to have the baby in my eyes, and to me that's totally wrong. Given a few ideas either way on what a girl should do, I think family and friends should support her on her own decision.

I've noticed a lot of difference in Lesley. She's more confident now. She'll go and talk to people, sort things out for herself, say with the Social or something. Living at home it was all arranged for her. They even filled in forms for her. She was never left to do it for herself. I think she's realised she's a person and not somebody to do the bidding of other people. I'll tell her to do something and she says, "Do it yourself!" Her Dad treats her more like an adult now, asks her to do things now instead of telling her. Little things like that have changed. Lesley probably doesn't even realise, but I can watch it.

And I've changed a lot, with the baby. I've become close to Lesley, closer to the baby, and I'm more careful with money. I was atrocious before with money. I realise now it's not just my money anymore. I suppose I am more responsible as well. But any other way I've not changed. I've been away from my part of the family since I was fifteen. I've seen more of life than the majority of people my age. I think I settled down a few years back. The only big difference in lifestyle is having a baby.'

2

PARENTS: REACTIONS AND RELATIONSHIPS

After the first feelings of shock turn into either joy or dismay, the question that immediately arises is, 'How do I tell Mum and Dad?' It sometimes seems like an impossible thing to do. It usually depends on the relationship that girls already have with parents – and mothers in particular. If you have a good and close relationship with your mother you should be able to talk to her, but sometimes things are not even as straightforward as this, and if you are close to someone who you know is going to be upset or disappointed in you, it may be even harder to do. Therefore you don't say anything for a while, conceal it, perhaps even kid yourself that the pregnancy will go away if you don't acknowledge it. Perhaps the moment is never right, there's always some excuse. You don't want to spoil Christmas, or it's your sister's birthday, or you're afraid of your mum's temper.

Bridget concealed her pregnancy from everybody until she was about four months when she told her boyfriend, who was not the baby's father. Eventually it was he who told her mother when she was about eight months pregnant: 'We'd been planning it for ages to tell them but we hadn't had the nerve to get round to it. We were petrified. A couple of months before, my Dad said if I ever did get pregnant he'd chuck me out, so I thought they would.' Although her mum was upset and her dad was cross they didn't chuck her out but have been very supportive and she still lives at home with her two-year-old son.

It's also a source of distress to parents that their daughters couldn't feel able to confide in them, but it happens. It may not just be because of the reactions girls fear from their parents, but also because of the mental block they themselves create, illustrated in this chapter by Joanne. One thing emphasised by every girl here who had delayed telling her parents about her pregnancy was that looking back, each wished she'd told them earlier, since the consequences were never as bad as she'd feared.

Parents may feel upset whatever the age of their teenage daughter, but those with younger daughters are obviously going to react more negatively than those with older teenagers. An eighteen- or nineteen-year-old is usually much more mature than a fourteen- or fifteen-year-old, and may even be contemplating marriage by this time. I found that most parents were initially rather shocked at finding out their daughter was pregnant, some cried, some got angry, some were very matter-of-fact, and some were quite pleased. But most were, sooner or later, very supportive. Often they wanted only what seemed best for their daughters, and some are prepared to set aside strong religious beliefs for this. Judy's father, for instance, despite being a devout Catholic would have encouraged her to have an abortion if she had wanted one. Some parents, whether openly or secretly, may feel quite pleased at the prospect of being grandparents.

Sometimes there did seem to be different reactions from mothers and from fathers. Mothers often had an immediate and emotional response, anger or tears, but this was often quickly resolved into practical and psychological support. There are always the exceptions, mothers who remain distant and angry, or who actually tell their daughters to leave. But in general, parents love their daughters, and are very concerned about them and their welfare. Fathers too may respond in a positive way, but I definitely felt that fathers tended to have a more extreme reaction of anger of hurt, or said they were ashamed of their daughter, and felt let down, and some refused to speak to their daughters for days or weeks. Girls were often far more scared of telling their fathers than their mothers, and mothers were often given this task. Diane locked herself in her bedroom and wouldn't come down for a day because she was afraid of her father's anger. Sandra's father also reacted strongly.

> I had just turned sixteen. My mother told my father and I think that must have been the worst time of my life. My father went mad and I think he actually hated me for a short while. He said he didn't want to see my baby, and that I had to go into a home for unmarried mothers. It was my mother who stuck up for me and in the end he came around and now him and my baby are inseparable.

Fathers may have very strong views on what course of action their daughters should take. Lesley, for instance, had kept her baby because her father said if she had an abortion she wouldn't be considered part of his family anymore. Mary's father was frosty with her because she didn't have an abortion, right up until she brought her son back from the hospital. Some of this paternal anger is also rooted in the loss or 'violation' of father's 'little girl', and the recognition that she has become a sexually active person with a man of her own. Actually seeing her physically pregnant may increase this response, and so when she has had her baby and gone back to her usual size, it is easier to relate to her as a daughter again. Men are very protective and sometimes possessive towards their daughters and often find it hard to 'lose' her to another man.

However, whatever the initial reaction, a significant number of the girls thought that in fact their relationships with either their mother or their father, or both, had actually improved since they had had their baby. Sometimes it was through being treated as more grown-up, more mature, not a child anymore. Now they and their mothers could share more things because they had been through the same experiences – something that happens with older mothers and their parents as well. This is what Helen had found:

My relationship with my parents had never been close. I never confided in them about anything except school or college. Mum and I are much closer now. I can talk to her in a way I couldn't before and she's been a great help over the past year. I wouldn't have got through it without her. Dad, on the other hand, is steadily getting further away. We've never been close and my getting pregnant hasn't helped at all.

Folasade felt she had changed in that having a baby had given her more confidence and put her on a more equal footing with her mother.

We've always been close, but we've got a different relationship now. Before it was cheeky girl and mother. Now it's mother and experienced daughter. I can say what I like. I don't have to hide the fact that I'm sleeping with Michael. I can talk to her about things. If one's got something beneficial to say, they'll accept it readily, whether it's mother or daughter. Whereas before the advice flowed one way, it all came from my mum.

Studies of young mothers have found that history tends to repeat itself within a family, and teenage mothers tend to have children who in turn become teenage parents themselves. This was the case with a significant number of the girls talking here, for instance, Lorraine and Cathy, both of whose mothers had had children in their teens, and consequently had felt very sympathetic to what their daughters were going through, and Debbie's mother, who had been more upset because she did not want her daughter to have the same sort of life as she had had.

How easy or difficult it is for girls to tell their parents that they are pregnant also depends on how accustomed they are to confiding in their mothers or fathers about periods, boyfriends, sex and contraception. Only a few girls told me that these matters were ever discussed within their families. The others said that they had gained what knowledge they had elsewhere.

Living with the family

Bringing the baby back home to the family heralds the start of another sort of life. If the baby's grandmother is young and has young children herself, they may all be brought up together, just like one generation. Tracy lives with her mother and their young daughters, born within twelve months of one another. They go out together, babysit for one another, and sometimes get mistaken for friends or sisters taking their children out.

Sometimes the baby may be cared for mainly by its grandmother, so that its young mother can carry on leading her teenage life. Bridget looked after her son for the first eighteen months before getting a job so he recognises her as his mother, whereas it could be quite easy for a baby to start calling its grandmother 'Mum'. Joanne, however, goes out to work during the day and is out nearly every night, while her mother looks after her eight-month-old daughter, so they spend little time together.

Whereas this involvement by grandmothers is welcomed by their daughters, conflict can arise when a mother tends to 'take over' the care of her grandchild, telling her daughter what to do, how to do it, what to buy and so on. This may be done with the best intentions, but it can lead to frustration and arguments. In Diane's case, her mother had bought most of her baby things and also her maternity clothes. She found trying to be responsible mother, dependent daughter and 'normal young person' a source of constant conflict between her and her mother.

> My mum expects me to take all the responsibilities like feeding him and things but I don't get to buy his food. For instance, I wanted to feed him on the baby food in jars and I keep telling her I do, but I end up feeding him the powdered food like my mum wants. It seems to me she makes all the rules and I'm expected just to carry them out and still be responsible.

But overall, where girls were still in close contact with their parents, which the majority were, they were strong in praise of all the invaluable support and help, both financial and emotional, that they had got from them.

JOANNE

Joanne is a lively, dark-haired nineteen-year-old, with an eight-month-old daughter. She lives with her parents in a comfortable house overlooking fields and trees on the edge of a provincial Midlands town. She hated school and left at sixteen to go and train in a riding stables to be an instructor. Her daughter is even named after one of the horses she'd nursed there.

She developed a complete mental block against her pregnancy, and concealed it until four days before she went into labour. Her boyfriend was not interested and later denied that she had told him anything about it. She left the riding stables and went on the dole. Her parents never suspected she was pregnant but rather worried that she was ill with some other condition. They had recently had to cope with her elder sister becoming pregnant. Despite being rather shocked, they responded extremely well, and gave Joanne a lot of help and support.

Joanne had carried on with normal life as best she could, even going to discos at seven months pregnant, and all-night parties. Because she did not have any preparation for pregnancy or birth, her labour and delivery were quite difficult, complicated by her having curvature of the spine which was not realised at such short notice.

Her boyfriend, having disappeared during her pregnancy, returned and acted like a concerned father for a few months after the baby was born, even coming to live in Joanne's house, but then left as suddenly as he had come, and all the family feel very bitter about this.

For a few months Joanne stayed at home, but became desperate to get a job and regain her independence. Her mother was willing to look after the baby, so she got a fulltime job as a teacher's assistant in a mental home. She also reestablished a fairly active social life in the evenings, again using her mother as a babysitter. Although Joanne clearly loves her daughter very dearly and feels that having her has made her more responsible, she spends relatively little time with her. However, Joanne and her parents agree that having the baby has brought them all closer together as a family, and it has provided a focus and role for her mother, who, after Joanne's account, tells her version of the way that this has positively transformed her life.

'Mum used to send me down to the job centre for jobs. I used to sit outside the job centre, then come home and say, "I have applied, but I had to send in an application form", and I hadn't even gone in there. She used to say, "Get some weight off you, get a job and get some weight off you." It was funny because to start with I lost that much weight, because I wasn't eating. Then the weight started coming on. First of all Mum thought I was anorexic and then she thought I'd got thyroid trouble.

My sister had that. My dad used to sit here and say "Why don't you go to the doctors?" But I just ignored him and watched the telly. That would get him annoyed and we'd all end up fighting. A few times I sat down in the kitchen and almost told mum but changed my mind. I just couldn't do it. I think I've always found it hard to talk to people, except for my best mate. But I've never really talked to my mum about anything. I knew straightaway after the first month. So I told Tim. "Get rid of it," he said. "I'll pay." It's the only thing he has offered to pay for. I wish I'd taken the money now! Finding I was pregnant scared me more than anything. Because my sister Vanessa was also pregnant and saying to me, "I'm pregnant, what am I going to do?" I thought, here we go, two of us. Who's going to tell mum first. She told Mum, and the reaction she got from Mum – I thought I can't cope with this. So I kept it to myself.

I told my best friend to start with, and she said "For God's sake, I'll book you in down the doctors." I said no, I wouldn't go. The one thing I did not want was an internal. I think that was half the reason why I didn't go down the doctors. To stop her going on at me I said, "No, I'm not." Then I stopped seeing her. I dropped all my mates, dropped everybody. I got to the stage where I wasn't coping any more. I just had a complete mental blockage. I think I was sick about twice, and that was it. I just forgot it. I was still going and getting the shopping for my mum and looking after my sister's baby as she couldn't cope because he was a naughty little boy. I was carrying him upstairs in his pram thing, with only about a week to go. I thought it might go away. I think, looking back on it, I really did. I used to cry myself to sleep every night, hoping Mum wouldn't come in. It obviously showed, but I wore big baggy clothes. The first thing Mum did when she found out was throw them all away. It got to the stage where me and Mum were coming to blows. Just because I

wouldn't say anything. I felt really guilty afterwards.
She said, by the shape of me she wanted to ask me, but she
didn't want to in case she offended me. So I just went and
told my sister. I said I was eight-and-a-half months. She
phoned up the doctors and said she'd make an appointment
for me. Then she came down here to tell my mum. My
mum rang me up and said, "Look, everything's going to be
all right." She said come down and we'd sort my dates out.
Then my dad's car was here, and the first person who came
out was my dad and he came and put his arm round me.
They were really good, if I'd known I'd have told them
sooner. They were fine with me, and funny with my sister.
That's what really put me off. If my dad went up the wall
with that, what was he going to do with me? But they were
completely different. Perhaps because the circumstances
were so different. They let me wear a maternity dress then,
because I hadn't worn one up till then. The thing that
upsets me when I see all these pregnant people walking
around is that I didn't do it. I never really was officially
pregnant. I didn't wear maternity clothes. I didn't do
anything, and I didn't feel pregnant. I'd walk down town
with Vanessa, and she'd be looking at baby clothes, and
I'd think, Oh God. I wasn't interested. Whereas usually I
would be. It upset me really to think that I just wasn't
interested. I think it upset her as well. She was really
enthusiastic. I wasn't keen on babies, I'm still not now. I've
never been child minded. It's always been animals.

I didn't really want to start a relationship like that. We
both got a bit drunk, and it was just the way it was. Just
happened. I regretted it straight after. But it was too late
then. It was my one and only time. And I won't get
pregnant again. That's it now. Sixteen hours in labour.
Vanessa was there the whole time. All I kept asking for was
my dog. The gynaecologist who was there was fantastic.
I really knocked him about. I just got that scared, because

55

I'd never been to an antenatal class, I didn't know what was going to happen. I didn't even read a book on it, I just shut out that much. I used to be a punk. It's Tamara that's calmed me down. Used to have my bondage clothes, and the hair. I don't think I could now. I wouldn't do it, for her. I'd never walk round town looking like I used to. But it's still nice to go out and enjoy myself. Nightclubs and things, and stop at my friends. I've become more outgoing since. Stuff the world, I'm going to enjoy myself. I think this is because for the last five months I was pregnant, I was so withdrawn and wouldn't talk to anybody, wouldn't go out of the house, I used to sit upstairs or here hoping she wouldn't kick too hard and my dad wouldn't see anything. Hoping he wouldn't ask me to turn the telly over and I'd have to get up. But my friends really got me out afterwards, they came round and took me out. Got me back into the swing of things. I think I forgot how to enjoy myself.

Mum looks after Tamara. I pay her housekeeping, and I buy her things. I do feel guilty about it sometimes. She cooks the teas and does the housework and everything. If I'm here I try and help. I'm always rushing around doing things. I've never been very good at it, but I do try. Mum's really been fantastic. It's made her look much better, she's put on weight, and stopped smoking. She was smoking for twenty-five years. I suppose it's because she's got something else to think about now. Before she used to sit and worry because she had nothing to worry about. My dad's like me, he's never been really over-impressed with kids, but he's good. He'll sit and play with her and talk to her. And he realises I'm not a child anymore. Before I used to have to rebel to get my own way. Now I just say, I'm doing it. And he says, yes all right. They've never been hard on me on times to come in and that, but he's great now. I come in when I want. As long as I get up in the morning. Before, I was the youngest, and he didn't approve.

Tamara's the best thing that's happened to me. I feel very close to her, but I'm never here. Now I spend a bit more time with her because I don't go out to work until later, before I was starting at seven. I've become more open, and I think in a way it has made me grow up. When I'm with her I'm more responsible. I was completely irresponsible before. I couldn't care less about anything before. Although I don't feel I've changed much because I'm doing exactly the same things. But when I go out she's the only thing I talk about, she's more important. I don't really think of myself as a mother. A lot of people don't believe she's mine. I'm still young. I still want to go out, do what I want. I know it's my fault she's here, I suppose in a few years time I'll wish I'd been here, but now I want to be out enjoying myself.

I would never advise anybody to keep it to themselves. Get it out in the open. There's nothing worse than keeping something like that to yourself. It cracked me up terrible. I didn't really know what was happening. I used to lay there absolutely amazed when she moved inside me. I couldn't believe it. I used to poke her to move her round. That was the only time I really enjoyed it. Four o'clock in the morning she used to move about. I couldn't believe there was something alive inside me. It's funny, I didn't appreciate the fact that I was putting on weight. I saw myself as thin, and not pregnant at all. Now I realise I must have looked awful. Three other girls I've spoken to said they didn't tell their mums till they were six months pregnant. They had to tell them because they started showing. I'll never know how I did not tell anybody. I couldn't do it again.'

JOANNE'S MOTHER

'**E**very other mother has said, well if it was my daughter, I'd have known. But I never once thought. I really thought she'd got kidney trouble, or thyroid trouble. But I couldn't get her to the doctor, she wouldn't go. At first she kept passing out and she was sick. I thought oh no, she's gone on to a vegan diet. She's got anorexia. And then she got fatter and fatter. And she looked dreadful. She must have gone through hell every day, because we kept on to her how fat she was, how ugly she was. It wasn't at all like her. We were worried sick about it. And very upset that she looked so awful, because we always thought she looked so lovely. Even if she was punky, she was lovely. Then suddenly she had no make-up, she was fatter, drooping about. She wore boots, all through the summer. Her legs were so swollen, she had to cover them up.

Then she told her sister, who came down in a taxi and I was talking to a woman who would not get off the phone. Poor Vanessa was stabbing a cigarette, a cup of tea, another cigarette, hopping from one foot to the other. When I came off the phone she said, "Mum you'd better sit down. I've something terrible to tell you." I thought, oh, her and Colin. They'd only been married months, I thought they'd had their first row and she'd come home. Then she said, "It's Joanne, she's pregnant." I said, "When is it due?" "Now." I thought she was joking. As she said that, so dad arrived in the car with my mum, who is an absolute prude, and my auntie. I got the rest of it out of Vanessa, and I said I had to tell them now. It would probably kill my mum but I had to tell them. They all came in, they'd had a lovely day shopping. I told Mum to sit down, and I just said, "Joanne is pregnant. It's due now. What are we going to do?" I went and phoned the doctor, and he said bloody hell, what are you going to do? I said that's why I'm phoning you. We had to get her into hospital quick. And we spent all day in maternity ward. We went through all the books, a crash course literally. Nine months rolled into hours. I felt shattered. We just didn't get time to think. We had just four days. Luckily. If I'd had time to think I don't know how I would have felt. But if I'd had eight months of thinking, I don't think I could have taken it. As it happens, she couldn't be better.

The baby's so good. And she's made such a difference to me. Mentally. The doctor has said to me that since she came I'm changed completely. I no longer need sleeping tablets, I no longer need the occasional valium. I don't smoke any more. I'm just completely relaxed, and I'm not tense any more. I'd begun to think I'd got this agorophobia whatever it is, I never wanted to go out. I have to tell myself that she's not mine. And I know that one day she will go, and then what will I do? This is what the health visitor keeps saying to me. Don't get too attached. Joanne must look after her own baby. One day she'll break your heart. But Tamara is such a happy, nice, pleasant baby. And if I made Joanne stay in, she would be so miserable, that it would make the baby miserable. So what's the best thing? Joanne can't sit still long enough to feed her, but I love it. We agree on more or less everything. The only thing Joanne really doesn't like is her pretty dresses. I used to hate taking her out in a track suit. She should have pretty dresses and frilly pants on.

Dad was very upset that she hadn't confided in us. He felt that she should have cared enough to confide in us, where really she cared too much and didn't. Now he thinks more of her than he did of these, when they were babies. He pays much more attention to her. He plays with her, talks to her. She's had a positive effect on the whole family. It's totally different to my own children. I seem to have more time for her than I had with them, and I still do my housework and all the washing. I haven't got the rush, somehow. I don't know what it is, but it's different, bringing her up to what it was bringing them up. It's very hard for parents. Joanne really has been hard work, right from the day she was born. She was awful at school. It was nothing to be sent for by the headmaster. I don't know whether she's changed or not, she's got an awful lot of growing up to do. She's not responsible for Tamara at all. She's got to be out and about with her friends. You can't do that with a baby. She thinks nothing of going out at ten o'clock at night. How can you if you've got a baby? If she didn't do it, she would blow up, I'm sure. Which is why we say, if she has to go out, do it.'

NICKIE

Nickie, aged eighteen, lived with her parents, who had come to Britain from the West Indies in the 1950s, until she was sixteen. Then she had been forced to leave when it was discovered that her real father was a white man. The father she had always known would no longer have anything to do with her so she had eventually got a tiny room in a house in London which served as a hostel for single girls.

She had a good job working with an airline company until she became pregnant after missing just one day of taking the Pill. Neither her mother and 'father', nor her white boyfriend were pleased at the news. When she was about three months pregnant, and feeling totally rejected by everyone, she got into a very depressed state, staying in her room for several days without moving, wondering if this was what it was like to be dead. Then she brought herself out of it. At the same time her mother came to visit her, her boyfriend appeared again, and things started looking up.

However, she went into labour eleven weeks early, and

*her baby daughter went into intensive care, where she still
was when she talked to me. At this time there seems little
chance of Nickie getting rehoused into her own flat, which
is her main dream in life. Meanwhile, the only alternative
seems to be for the baby to be looked after by her mother,
and she will go and visit in the evenings when her 'father'
has gone off to his night work. Although her twenty-six-
year-old boyfriend has an income from his job managing a
shop, he has so far taken little interest and no responsibility for her or the baby. He just comes round once in a
while and they go out.*

*She is finding life very tough and depressing, stuck in
her room, her baby in hospital, with little hope on the
horizon of a proper home or family life. She is quite bitter
about what has happened, resentful at what she sees as the
inconsistent attitudes towards pregnancy and teenage
motherhood held by members of her family and other West
Indian people and still upset at her 'father's' extreme
change in attitude towards her when he found out she was
not his daughter.*

'This all began when I was fifteen. My brother and
sister, they're very very dark. I used to say to my
mum, "Why am I this colour?" Mum said, "Oh well, it goes
back to your ancestors. I had a grandmother that was half-
caste." My dad started saying to my mum, "What's this?"
And because I kept on asking, my dad started getting a bit
funny. I came back from school one time, and my brother
said, "Stay outside". I thought, something's up with my
mum, and I went in the house. I said, "What's happening?"
and my dad went like this, right across my face, and I went
flying over the table. After all these years I thought the
man in our house was my dad, and he wasn't. It upset me a
lot. Before my dad was really good to me, but after that it
changed. I'd come in from school and he wouldn't say hello

to me. Mum would dish up my plate of food, and I'd go and sit down with it, and he'd get up. So I left, and went to stay at a friend's. Then I came back. My mum said to me, "You've left once, you might as well stay out." He doesn't speak to me. He's told friends, "All these years I've thrown away money on that child." He's proud of his grand-daughter, but he won't have anything to do with me.

My brothers and sisters knew my dad could harbour a grudge, but not like this. I mean, we've lived together since we were young babies, and to them it's nothing. To me, they're still my brothers and sisters. They don't care, because they know me. But my dad, he will just not accept it. And to make matters worse, it was a white guy my mum had an affair with. I think that made it worse, my dad said you can't mix, in this world, you should have white, Indian and black. You shouldn't mix. A lot of people think you shouldn't mix. When Robert and I first met, it was, "Oh dear". They just think it's wrong, it's the worst thing you could do. I've got aunties with daughters married to white guys, and they will not accept the guy. Some of them will just forget the guy and just relate to the daughter. Others will just forget that they have a daughter completely, just for the reason they're married to a white guy. Just cut them off completely. I was down the market with this other girl, and we saw her mum there. I said hello, and she was all right to me, but not the girl. It was like they were strangers, and they're mother and daughter. I really don't know why it's so wrong. When they first came to this country – like my mum, when she first came she said she couldn't find a place to live because people didn't want black people on their premises. I say to her, "Forgive and forget, because times have changed." I'm not saying people aren't racist, but things have changed. People accuse the whites of being prejudiced, but blacks can be just as bad.

With Robert's mum – to start with it was fine. Then it just got worse and worse. And his dad – oh my God. I didn't say "Hi" to him, I said "Hello, good evening". And it was like I wasn't there. Like I was just a shadow, or a dog he doesn't have to talk to. And at first his mum said, "Don't bring that girl in my house." Then she invited me to dinner. But his dad just wouldn't have anything to do with me. It's weird, because before all this happened, I thought this country was great – but people have got really bad attitudes, and no matter what anybody else says, they'll just stand by their beliefs, they will not change. If I took Robert home, mum would say "Don't bring him in, what you bringing him for?" And then my friends' boyfriends, on an evening out, they used to just have a go at him, and I'd feel really embarrassed. They'd tease him about everything.

He was glad when I got pregnant to start off with, but he's changed. He was glad because – well, not having kids before, he only thought about the nice side of being a dad, he didn't think about the bad side. We had a little bit of money, we wanted all these things for the baby, but he couldn't afford the money. His image of being a father was different. He thought, this isn't the way I thought it would be. So now he just comes round once in a blue moon. I didn't think he'd do that, because we'd had problems before, because of the black and white thing, There's a lot of people who will just stop you in the street. He didn't mind that at all, he argued for me. And if I'd had any problems, he sorted them out. So I didn't think because he's got pressure, with the baby situation, that he'd go. But he did. And we were very much together, and in love.

My family are just so typical. The mother will have a kid, not necessarily with another man, but they'll have kids before they're married. Like my aunties. Some of them had babies before they were married. Some had kids when they were fourteen and fifteen. And then you get yourself pregnant and they treat you like it's a sin. It doesn't occur to them that they've done the same. I've pointed it out on many occasions. And if you say you did the same thing, they just think, oh my God, look at this girl being really rude. And then there's the attitude towards black girls with babies. They say, "These girls have no ambition, they just come out of school and make babies." That's the expression. They don't say "having" babies, they say "make babies". My mum was always saying, "All these girls making babies". They think white girls will get their house. My mum and aunt are always saying to me, a white girl will first of all be engaged, then marry, then live in her mum's house for a little while until they can afford the mortgage on their place, then buy a house, live there for a couple of years, then they'll have the baby. I say, "Mum, you're living in the dark ages. Not all girls do that." No, says Mum, a black girl leaves school, and as soon as she leaves school she'll start making babies. She wouldn't even rent a place, she'd just start making babies. That is just an attitude, and I don't know where they get that from. It's a bloody stupid attitude. There's a lot of white girls that get pregnant as well. These West Indian girls, they're living in their mum's houses, and they say, "Mum, I'm pregnant." Before that, these mums won't sit down and talk about contraceptives, you have to learn it all from the walls at school or from friends, because these parents aren't telling you. Then when you get pregnant it's "Lord Jesus Christ have mercy, you're pregnant, oh my God!" It's something bad, like you've got V.D. or something. They won't say, "I'll come to the clinic with you" or "I'll help you." Their immediate reaction is to kick them out, put their belongings on the doorstep and tell them to leave.

This has happened to my friends. And it's only when the child is two or three, or beginning to talk or whatever, that's when the mums come around. They go into bed and breakfast. And the boyfriend – when the mother kicks them out of the home – the boyfriend says, "Uh-oh, she's out on the street now, and pregnant." And away they go, some of them. So the girl has no family and no boyfriend. That happens to so many people. I think – all right, don't be happy about the situation if you don't want to be, but don't kick your daughter out on the street. They said to me when I was younger, "You become pregnant and you're going, you're not staying in the house." Sometimes the mum, after a couple of years, the mum will come around, but not the dad. First of all she'll start to do things behind the dad's back. Then she'll say, "Oh I'll look after the baby." My mum – she doesn't say the word sex, she thinks the word sex is dirty – she'll say, "When you get in a mix up" – that's what she calls it. I had to figure out what she was saying. When she was talking like that, I'd say, "Mum what are you talking about?" and she'd say, "Oh never mind, you won't understand." And you don't get any more. And so many of my friends have said the same. Their mums don't talk to them about contraceptives, or sex. They had to learn it from school. Or from people out on the street. But not from the parents indoors. A lot of them say, "Oh, my daughter's pregnant." It doesn't occur to them that if they had told them about contraceptives, they would not be pregnant. And many parents think, oh my daughter would not have sex. Therefore it's not necessary to tell her about contraceptives. And that's what makes them much more angry.

If I'd have my time over again, I'd do things so differently. I'd not have a child at my age. I'd rather use contraception, than know that I'm going to become pregnant. But now, after what happened, I'll not miss the Pill again. I've got this watch with an alarm on it, so that I know when to take it. I shan't risk forgetting again. I think it's harder, being black and having a baby. People's attitudes, they're so different. White friends that I've got, their mums argued at first, but now they're just bringing the baby up as their own. They're not arguing any more. With my black friends, their babies are two years old and the parents still cause so much strife. I don't know why. They've done the same thing. My friend Pauline, she has a daughter of eight, and her mother and father still aren't talking to her. My mum had my sister before she was married, when she was seventeen. If she had sat down and explained things to me, I don't care how long it took, it would have been something. A lot of the parents know what they're talking about, they've seen it all already, what we're going through. But they will not open up and talk. Some just don't want to reveal themselves when they were younger. Mum would tell us things about her childhood, and then come to a bit and just shut up. We'd say, "What happened next?" and she wouldn't say a word. She loves telling me "Prevention is better than cure", but she won't tell the rest.'

TRACY

Tracy is eighteen and lives in a little house in the west of England with her mother, who is forty-one, and both their daughters. Tracy's is two years old and her mother's daughter is three. Her parents divorced about ten years before. Her father lives quite close by, but they are not very close and she does not see very much of him. Tracy got pregnant on the day she left school. She got six CSEs of which two were grade ones. She wanted to be a hairdresser, and had even started a course, but consequently had to leave.

Her baby's father was quite a bit older than she, twenty-six, and wanted her to have the baby because he thought that having mumps had made him sterile. Tracy was persuaded, but as time went on, decided she didn't really want to be with him, so she left him. She soon fell in love with someone else, also about nine years older than herself, who seemed very keen and wanted to marry her. He was in the Navy and away a lot of the time. During the first six months after the baby was born he was very helpful when he was around, as Tracy sometimes felt she couldn't cope because her daughter cried so much. But soon after he had a change of heart and left her. Although she has had a few boyfriends since, there is no one special around. She became pregnant again about six months ago, through a contraceptive failure, but this time decided to have an abortion. Even though her boyfriend at the time was against this, she was determined not to be persuaded to have another baby.

Tracy is on social security but by living at home she even manages to save a little. She pays her mother housekeeping money, and her mother still tends to look after her. They are good friends, do quite a lot of things together with their two young children, and are sometimes mistaken for sisters.

'Mum knew I was sleeping with my boyfriend. People say she was lenient with me. I think she was frightened to be too strict. My mum and dad had been through a very bad divorce, so I suppose she was frightened of being too strict and pushing me away, in case I turned against her. She never encouraged me, but she didn't stop me. My dad blames my mum for the way things turned out for me. She came with me when I first went on the Pill. I was about fifteen. It was her idea. But it made me sick and dizzy, so I didn't take it. I wasn't sleeping with anyone, it was just in case. When I first slept with someone, I used Durex. Then I became allergic to Durex so I went back on the Pill. A different one. But I was bad again, so I came off it. Then I tried a different Durex, but I was allergic to them all. I just gave up. I didn't bother then.

People say having a baby ruins your life, and talk about what you could have done in a job and that. But I'll be young when she goes to school. I'll be young enough to get a job. I'll only be twenty-one or so then. I can still get training and get a job. Some people are older than that. When I'm thirty, Sally won't be far behind me, not such an age gap. Like me and my mum. She had me when she was twenty, and we're more like friends really. People think we're sisters sometimes. We go out together. Other girls at school used to think that was funny, because they never talked to their mums and didn't even know how old they were. One of my friends thought she was pregnant and she told my mum before her own mum. I do everything with my mum. She's forty-one now, but she's young. She looks young for her age and she acts young. People think of her as younger. When people know she's a grandmother they're amazed. It's the way you dress and act. She's jolly and up to date. And because she's got a little girl, people think we're friends or sisters.

Mum looks after Sally sometimes for me. But mostly I just don't go out. If my mum wants to go out, or goes to work, I stay at home and look after the girls, and vice versa. We don't often get a babysitter unless we want to go out together. People ask me sometimes, why don't I get a flat and live on my own with my little girl? But I don't want to. I like living with my mum and her little girl. She does too. So what's the point of us moving out? We get on well. We have arguments, everyone does. But not often. The only thing is that the little girls fight. They're terrible.

I don't see my dad very often at the moment, unless I actually go up there. He's got his own business and shop.

Sally knows who he is though, although he's never looked after her. I wish he would, but he's never offered. My sister-in-law is just about the same age as me, and I don't know whether it's because they're married or whether it's because she's not his daughter, but he treats her completely different. I think he thinks of me still as more of a child. He won't talk to me about sex, or boyfriends or anything. I won't talk to him about it either.

I would say to other pregnant teenagers that I think it's great if they are happy about it. But I was talked into it by my boyfriend. I don't think you should be talked into anything. I should have done what I wanted. I suppose I was confused at the time. But I'd say, just do what you want to do, nothing else. Whatever it is. I was lucky, my mum was good, she didn't threaten to throw me out or anything. Now I get social security and my family allowance. I give my mum money for housekeeping and that. She buys all the food, and pays for the laundry. If we go out we take it in turns to pay. She does the shopping, and the cooking she does too. She's still like my mum. We share the housework. I don't suppose I'd manage that well if I was on my own. I suppose you get used to it, but at the moment I haven't got to do it. When Sally was born, she knew I wanted to look after her myself. She helped but she didn't tell me what to do all the time. She advises me but she doesn't take over at all. She'll say "Why don't you try it this way?" and not, "Do it this way."

I think it's made me grow up. I think I feel older than my age, and I suppose I do act older in a way. You realise more what life's about. If I was younger, I think I'd have still had her. But now when I think about it, I think maybe I wouldn't. It's hard to say. But I can't imagine being without her, so I don't really regret it.'

3
SCHOOL AND EDUCATION

If you are pregnant and under the age of sixteen, it is compulsory that you receive some sort of education until you reach this age. There are three main ways you can do this; you can continue at school, have a home tutor, or attend a special unit or project set up for pregnant school-girls and school-age mothers. The school year runs from September to August and whether sixteen-year-olds can continue at school or leave if they wish depends when their birthday falls. This makes it quite difficult to get accurate figures about school-age mothers. About two-thirds of the mothers in this book were at school or further education college when they became pregnant, and about half of these were under sixteen.

The option of staying at school or returning after the birth of the baby is often not a very popular one. Indeed some schools do not allow girls to do this, seeing pregnancy, like measles, as infectious. For girls themselves, it may also be a daunting prospect, especially if they're feeling rather vulnerable and embarrassed about their condition. Other girls and boys can be very unkind, as Doreen had found: 'All the kids kept pointing fingers, talking behind my back, starting rumours and were generally very bitchy.' She left after a few months and had a home tutor. Bridget too had a similar experience: 'The other girls had mixed feelings, some of them were happy for me but some thought I was a slag and a tart and that I didn't know who the father was, and they were bitchy towards me when they passed in the corridors.'

Lyn went into school at fifteen when she was almost due to give birth. She was wearing big maternity clothes and felt 'dead weird' being with everyone else in school uniform. It was break time and everyone was in the yard, talking about her:

> They won't come up to you because they think you're dirty, because you got pregnant and you're only fourteen or fifteen, but if you're seventeen or eighteen it doesn't matter, you're old. But because you're still at school they think you're dirty and disgusting and they call you a slag, but it could happen to them any day.

Rachel remembers walking into school assembly the first time, after everybody had found out.

> I walked into assembly and everybody turned round and they didn't look at me, they looked at my stomach, everybody in that hall. I was with my three mates and they stood behind me and said, 'I don't see why you should be ashamed.' but I wouldn't go in after that, it was really horrible. They don't call you names, what they do, they hurt you more by not asking you, but asking your friends, 'Is she pregnant?' You've thousands of mates until you have a baby and then you discover who your real friends are.

These were both common complaints: that other girls or boys did not have the nerve to ask you to your face if you were pregnant or not, and that 'you find out who your real friends are'. Friends stand or fall by whether they stick by you and still see you when you have your baby and cannot go out much anymore.

It may be easier for someone who is a bit older. Folasade, for example, left school without anyone knowing she was pregnant, and then returned to the sixth form after having her baby, to take her A-levels.

Before I got pregnant it was taken for granted I'd be in the sixth form, then when I found out, I thought I had two months to tell everybody I won't be back and they're going to say, 'How come?', so I was saying, 'Oh God, I'm going to fail my O-levels, you won't see me back here again'. Then I came back, O-levels and baby and all.

I didn't know what to expect when I came back to school. It must have been halfway through the year, and it was – 'You were pregnant! I couldn't believe it!' I got asked about it for months. I had a permanent grin on my face about it all. I like talking about Baby. Everybody talked to me in the corridor. After the initial, 'God, you've had a baby!', everything was normal, my friends didn't treat me any different really.

Teachers would come up smiling – not having spoken to me since the first year and now I was a sixth former. Sometimes things would happen, like when I first started potty training her. I used to have Physics at half-nine and every now and then she'd have an accident in the road so I'd be running home, changing her and taking her back to nursery, which would mean I'd be half an hour late. So this was the reason I was late and then it was, 'Sit down, all right'. At first it was very good, I couldn't do anything wrong because I had a baby.

The teachers treat me as an adult, but I've always been very mature for my age. The one I mostly chat to is the biology teacher. She had her first child, then I had mine, and then she had her second child. So we bring photographs in.

Although girls may be understandably reluctant to expose themselves to the stares and comments of other girls and boys, their views and experiences of contraception and motherhood could be very relevant and helpful to others of their own age who are still at school. Without taking adequate precautions, they too could be in the same situation themselves by the end of the year.

The option of having a home tutor is often quite successful. It is at the discretion of local education authorities to offer pregnant schoolgirls and school-age mothers a number of hours free home tuition per week. London, for example, will provide ten hours a week, for schoolchildren eligible under certain categories. Pregnancy falls under 'medical grounds'. Girls either go to a local centre for tuition, or to the tutor's home, or are taught within their own homes. In London this continues for six weeks after the baby's birth, after which girls are encouraged to go back to school. Tuition may be continued on special grounds. Several teenage mothers in this book had had a home tutor and most had enjoyed it. The one-to-one teaching usually meant that they learned more and did better than they would have in the classroom. Some of them had not attended school very regularly before. Often the tutor became more like a friend than a teacher, and continued to keep contact with them even after their period of education together had finished. Cathy had been assigned a tutor, she used to take her daughter along to a little school (not her previous school) and have lessons there in the staffroom:

I never liked school before but I liked this as it was only half-past nine till half-past twelve so it wasn't a long day and I could take Rebecca with me. I used to have a load of homework to take home with me because I had to catch up but I didn't used to mind that. It gave me something to do as well. I got better results than if I'd stayed at school. If I'd been at school I think I'd have wanted to leave at Easter. They wanted me to do O-levels but I said no. It would have been too much, having to look after Rebecca. I got five CSEs and grade 2s.

This system can also work for older teenagers, but if you are over sixteen you are not entitled to free tutoring. After Judy became pregnant in the lower sixth at school, she left and found herself a tutor for her A-level English, and also attended maths classes at the local college. She had to pay for tutoring out of her supplementary benefit, but it was well worth it as she enjoyed her studies, did well, and is still friends with her tutor.

The third option is to attend one of the special projects that exist in various cities. I visited two of these, the Arbour Project in Liverpool, and the Barkerend Unit in Bradford. The Arbour Project operates from a converted two-bedroomed flat above a shop in Liverpool. As well as providing pregnancy counselling to any girl at school up to the age of eighteen years, its ongoing work is to look after the social and educational needs of a small group of six or seven pregnant schoolgirls or school-age mothers who attend the unit every weekday for a period of twelve months. There are three full-time workers – a counsellor, a teacher, and a nursery nurse. There is also a health visitor who comes in to teach on the childcare course and to discuss any health problems, and a doctor who visits monthly to give innoculations and deal with any other aspects of health care. The project is jointly funded by several bodies, the main support coming from the education and social services departments. It has an open referral system, so girls can be recommended by their schools, educational welfare officers, maternity hospitals, and a variety of other sources, or they can come along on their own initiative.

These places clearly provide an invaluable experience for teenage mothers in which they receive education and social support. Although to some extent girls are cushioned from the outside world, it is probably a good thing at this time, and the advantages of attending such a project far outweigh any disadvantages. It is a great pity that there is not more provision of this kind. As it is, the number of girls that Arbour can take has to be limited in order to provide a good service within the constraints of the accommodation, and the number of staff. A girl will start coming to the project when she is pregnant, and come back after she has had her baby. It runs on the basis of a four-day academic week. Every Thursday is given over to a drop-in day, which is open to the previous year's group to come back or to any girl on home-teaching, and sometimes girls from three or four years back may also drop in for a chat or advice. After the intensive twelve months support with the project, girls need somewhere to come with any problems that may occur later. It is during this subsequent period that many problems arise, such as relationships with parents and living at home.

Girls clearly get a lot from attending the Project. They are taught a broad range of subjects, they learn about childcare and have a good preparation for motherhood, and they provide support and solidarity to each other. There are few rules laid down, apart from not smoking in the classroom and informing the staff if they can't come in, and the rest of the rules about things like washing up and cooking are made and implemented by girls themselves. Boyfriends are encouraged to visit, although not a lot of them do. The age range may run between thirteen and sixteen, but most girls are fifteen and have got pregnant in their fifth year at school. Girls usually leave Arbour after twelve months, having taken their exams, and any girls who, for instance, come in the third year at school are required to return to school afterwards. Therefore the unit also has to prepare them for reintegration into school life.

Educationally, girls work harder and do better than if they had still been in school. They are usually quite a mixed group, some of whom have had bad experiences at school or have been longterm truants. They all do exams, even if this is only the one in childcare. According to Hilary, the Project teacher:

> They are told they are coming here to carry on their education, and I interpret this as being very broad-based. I don't want to bring out a girl with six CSEs or 16+s who can't look after her baby, so you try to cater for the individual need. They usually come in until the day they have their baby, and most come back again very early, as soon as two weeks. And they're not coming back for their education; they're coming back for the support that Arbour gives them, so they may spend more time with Monica in the nursery looking after the baby and gradually they'll move back into the classroom in their own time and get back to their exams.
>
> On the whole they do very well in the exams. I think it's a reflection of their motivation, because I'm not a subject specialist. I could be doing eight or nine subjects so generally the girls are responsible for their education. They know what areas they've got to cover in maths or English and it's a question of their motivation. If they're in here working all day and everyday and they see the other girls taking exams and they know I'm going to make them work, quite often they'll take the exams because there's no point in not taking them, whereas I think if they were at home they would not have the same incentive. A lot of them actually do better for coming here. And I think another reason why we do so well educationally is that the baby gives them a sense of direction and purpose and they may not want to get 16+ exams but they want to for their baby.

Girls remain on the register of their previous schools, and take their chosen exams there, unless they do not wish to go back into school. In this case the Project becomes a temporary centre and they sit the exams there. Obviously very close relationships are built up through being in a small, close-knit group everyday, and this helps to carry girls through their work and exams. The workers are not just teachers or nursery nurses, their roles overlap and they are also more like friends than authority figures. This can be very helpful on both sides, as their advice can be asked and issues discussed in a way that girls may not be able to do with their parents or anyone else.

There is also a tremendous amount of shared support amongst girls themselves. For the pregnant girls it is often a real eye-opener to see the other girls go off, deliver their babies and come back, having survived it all. But then they also see exactly what is entailed in having a newborn baby to care for, who does not sleep all day, but cries and is sick and needs constant attention. They seem to come to terms with the reality of this much easier than a lot of other girls. In this respect, pregnant girls at Arbour are also very knowledgeable and confident about giving birth because they have been so well prepared for it, and tend to sail through labour and birth without a lot of problems. And some girls seem to change radically in personality after having their babies:

> You think you know a girl for six months and then she has a baby and becomes a completely different person. You get reports from school and it may say 'difficult' or whatever, but they may be a very different person in the pregnancy. They become very passive but as soon as they've had the baby they're back to their old selves again and you think, God, is it the same girl?

The girls at the Project talk with one another freely about their personal lives, and experiences and problems, and can describe and understand their situation better because they have become used to discussing it. Monica, the nursery nurse, told me:

They all know what it's like to come in and say, 'I hate that child, it's been crying all night; whereas they feel reluctant to say that to other people because people are looking at them and their age. It's quite normal for a mum to feel like that and they can talk to each other about it and support each other. And if things are going wrong at home, or with the boyfriend or the baby and a girl is really distraught, the others will rally round and make her coffee, take the baby and feed it, because they understand, and they feel for her. They can also talk very openly about sex and contraception, discussing any problems and giving one another advice. They're very good with each other's babies too, you can come in and not know which baby belongs to who, or a girl's got an exam coming up and they'll all muck in and change the baby for her.

It had been a really good experience for both Rachel, aged fifteen with an eleven-month-old baby, and Carol, aged fourteen and five months pregnant.

For me everything that's come out of Arbour's been good. I come in all the time, I'm never away. You can joke with them, have a laugh with them, it's just great. I've done my exams and I think I've done well in them. They've helped me with the baby, they take her away for a couple of hours a day, and they take you out to places – sports centres and hospitals. They show you how to do things, not like in the hospital where there's all mothers round you and nurses and they're all watching you. Here there's only Monica and she shows you how to do it and you get your confidence. And sometimes when you've had a late night with the baby and you come in and think, Oh, I've got to work, and they say if you're tired just go to sleep on the couch. At school you can't do that, and here you can have cups of tea.

It's nice to be among other mothers. You've got all the same things in common, you've all got a baby and you were all under-age when you had the baby and most of us done exams. And the amount of help you get the day before your exams – the same morning I turned round to Hilary after all the work she'd done with me and said, 'I'm going to fail, I'm not doing it.' And she said, 'Get in there and do it.' And when I started doing it I knew the hang of it and I turned round to her afterwards and said, 'That was easy.' I did six altogether.

You get told about Arbour by your school, or social worker or the hospital. When you first come in you feel dead funny because you're pregnant and they're all with kids and they're screaming and running round everywhere and you think, 'What have I got to put up with?' But you get used to it and I think it's a grand place, it's done me the world of good anyway, they don't half help you. I think you should make more effort to find out about places like this, and I think the schools should make an effort to tell you. It's good knowing that there's somewhere you can go for advice.   (Rachel)

It's helped me a lot. I'd rather be here than be at school. In school you'd be getting the looks and all that, but here everyone's in the same boat. And even if you still can talk to your mum after she knows, you've got someone here to talk to. It's easy here, Hilary, Monica and Yvonne are more like your mates than your mum, it's easier to talk to them than to talk to my mum. I used to babysit before but for older ones, and coming here's got me more used to younger babies. I'd never bottle-fed a little baby until I came here. You've got no say, you've got to do it and you get used to having a little baby, because after they're born they're not three or four, they're tiny. So you learn to cope with it.   (Carol)

Coming to the Arbour is not necessarily an easy option, despite its positive results. It requires girls to travel everyday, often across the city in all weathers. But for most of them it is clearly worth it, and Carol would struggle in even when she was not feeling well. And when the twelve months are over these young mothers usually go on to DHSS benefits, because they do not want to leave their babies and go to college or on YTS schemes. They have not got many choices open to them, and they are also very aware of people judging them as mothers because of their age, and feel that they constantly have to prove themselves.

After the exams are over, the Project takes the girls around to nurseries, parent support programmes, local sports centres, swimming and other activities. Although not strictly part of the academic programme, this is considered to be an important part of the project because if you enjoy your last experience of school, then you're more likely to return to studying something at a later stage in life. The relationship that develops between the girls and the workers is quite unique. Everyone's situation and problems get an airing and this does not mean any loss of respect, but more an insight into shared adult life. It is an educational setting that is totally unlike ordinary school, where girls learn to be responsible parents while also expressing themselves like any other fourteen- or fifteen-year-olds. They gain many things, from qualifications to self-awareness and confidence.

Barkerend is a similar unit that operates in Bradford, where there is no provision of home tuition, so pregnant school-age girls have only the choice of continuing at school or attending this unit. It is staffed by three fulltime teachers, and its aims are similar to the Arbour Project in that it provides continuing education, it takes girls through their pregnancies physically, educationally, emotionally and socially to produce healthy babies and mothers, and it tries to help girls achieve a level of maturity for taking on responsible parenthood. The age range runs between about twelve to seventeen years old, and there were twenty-four girls on the register at the time I visited the unit.

As every girl has her own individual subjects, the teaching is on a one-to-one basis, and each has cards showing her particular set work which has to be in at a certain time. The girls are required to plan their own day, and when they are used to this system, most prefer it to the structure of school and it gives them some control over their daily lives. They start at ten o'clock and finish at three with lunch from twelve to one o'clock. Any other breaks they organise themselves. They also have group activities when they learn about pregnancy and parenthood, do practical work, and discuss relevant issues and problems and how they might deal with these, if and when they may arise. Although a broad range of subjects is offered, the unit does not have the facilities for certain subjects such as science, so anyone wanting to do these subjects has to use the local college facilities instead.

Like the Arbour mothers, the Barkerend mothers have a very good record with the hospitals for having learned the language of pregnancy and birth. They know what to expect and what to ask for, and they tend to deliver extremely well. They too tend to work very hard, harder than they would have done at school, and get good results. At first girls may be preoccupied with their pregnancy or baby and see education as unimportant, but seeing other girls working soon builds their motivation. Although the unit obviously benefits girls who have tended either not to do very well in school, or who were regular truants, there is a tendency for more scholastically-minded girls to do worse educationally than they would have in school. The reason suggested for this is that these girls feel that they should be able to cope with their pregnancy and problems on their own instead of sharing them within the unit, as most other girls do. In trying to struggle on independently they have less time to concentrate on schoolwork.[1]

The unit lacks any proper creche facilities for the babies and therefore the girls take it in turns to look after them. They are often quite loathe to leave their babies with anyone else because, like many other young mothers, they are concerned to show the world that they are as good and responsible as any older mother. In this they have the basis to succeed, and one teacher noted after a drop-in day for former pupils:

> All those people who criticise these young girls and say they won't be able to cope and won't make good mothers ought to come in here and look at them now because they were absolutely fantastic with those children. The babies were developing properly and being well stimulated and doing the right things at the right age and they were really coping well.

Because they have been treated more as adults here, the contrast between this and ordinary school makes it sometimes difficult for them to return and adapt to being treated as children again, so it is obviously preferable for them to continue on at the unit.

The advantages of attending a unit of this kind or somewhere that gives similar solidarity and guidance has been shown in a study of schoolgirl mothers.[2] This found that girls who had felt isolated and embarrassed about being pregnant or having babies felt less stigma about this after they had attended the units and could take a much more realistic view of their situation. They benefitted both practically and emotionally compared to girls without such support, who suffered more from their lack of status and recognition as mothers. If there were more such places it would help to combat the cycle of deprivation that young mothers can get trapped in. A fifteen-year-old girl having her first baby is twice as likely to live at the poverty level than a nineteen-year-old first-time mother.

Returning to education at any time is not easy with small children, little money and few available childcare facilities, but it can be done. Sometimes if girls are living at home, they can reach some arrangement with one of the family to babysit while they go to further education college. Elaine was fifteen and at school when she got pregnant. Her mother had high hopes for her to take O-levels and go higher, so when she was pregnant, Elaine could not tell her because she felt she'd let her down. It was not until she was over seven months pregnant that her mother asked her if she was. Then they had to work out what to do.

> She'd thought everything through. She said, 'Do you want to put the baby up for adoption?' And I said, 'No, I don't want that.' So she said, 'Do you want me to adopt it and then I'll have all the responsibility and you can get on.' I said, 'No, I don't want that either.' She was willing to give everything up, but we talked it through and I said I could manage on my own. She said, 'You've got to promise me you'll go back to college and finish your education.' And I said, 'Yes, okay.' So we agreed and that was it, and I just got down to having Sam. Then I took a year off, and she kept going on and on at me that it's time to go back to college, so I did in the end. I'm taking a business studies course. I didn't want to go to begin with, but it was really good fun. Then it got quite boring, and it was really hard work, and now after the first year's finished I'm glad we thought of that because I've done quite well. I came top in my class this year and I'm glad she pushed me into it now.

Elaine left her son with her sister, who also had a young child, while she took her course. Helen left her daughter with her mother while she continued to take her A-levels at sixth form college. Kate's social worker organised nursery places for her two small children while she did her A-levels, and she has subsequently gone to a university where she can get creche facilities. Rosemary waited until her three children were at school before she started studying again. For any mothers wanting to go back to education, of whatever age, there are a variety of courses available, such as Fresh Start courses and TOPS courses. Some of them are run with creche facilities. If you feel that you have quite enough on your plate with a small child, then the idea of going back to education may not appeal, and many mothers I talked to said they had no such plans at present. They were happy to carry on taking each day as it came. But if and when you do want something else, going to college when you are older and when you positively want to go, can be a very different and more satisfying experience than being at school.

JUDY

Judy lives with her twelve-month-old daughter and her parents in their house in the north of England. At nineteen she is the youngest of four children and has always been treated as the 'little one'. She was in the sixth form at school starting her A levels when she met Andrew, the father of her baby. The night she got pregnant she had already been feeling depressed, and afterwards she immediately regretted what had happened. It had been her first time, she didn't love him, they didn't use any contraception and she definitely didn't expect to be pregnant as a result. The next time she saw Andrew she finished with him.

When she finally went to the family planning clinic, the woman she saw was not very sympathetic, 'she said "What school do you go to?" and when I told her she said "You've

*really thrown away your chances."' When the pregnancy
was confirmed she was in tears from the shock, even
though she had her suspicions when her periods failed to
arrive. It wasn't an easy prospect to tell her parents,
especially as her father was a strict Roman Catholic, but
this was forestalled by her mother coming across her letter
from the clinic. Both parents got very emotional and threw
their arms around her, although she had never felt they
were very close before.*

*She decided that she did not want to have either an
abortion, or to have the baby adopted. Andrew, when he
was told, denied responsibility and didn't want to know,
and has not been seen since. Determined to carry on with
her education, Judy got herself a tutor for her English,
and went to the local college to do maths. At the end of
two years she applied for jobs with various banks and when
I met her she had just been accepted as a trainee accounting technician. Having her daughter has not stopped her
from doing more or less what she had planned, but has
spurred her on to better results.*

'I had been off school since before my mum found out as
I had been sick with gastric 'flu. My morning sickness
I had explained away as the bug starting and a lot of the
time it was sickness at an evening meal. Because of this I
decided it wasn't worth going back to school so I just went
in to tell everyone and collect some books.

I was in the lower sixth, taking Maths, English General,
and Biology, so I dropped the Biology and took up English
with a tutor. I had the tutor for a year right until I took my
exams. It cost me money though, I originally got her from a
tutoring agency. I had to pay out of my supplementary
benefit, £7 an hour, just once a week. She did the English,
maths I did at the tech, which I got free as I was under
eighteen. That was Tuesday and Thursday from 6.30 to

9.00pm, it was a two-year course. I really enjoyed having a tutor and I learned more than if I'd been at school. You get it done more deeply at home, plus I did my homework properly. I'm still friends with my tutor, and she was really pleased when I told her I'd got a job. We ended up more as friends than tutor and pupil.

I've grown up since I left school. Everybody said that after I had Louisa I got a lot older, more mature. I didn't notice it myself but looking at the people at school you think how babyish. If I'd not had Louisa I don't suppose I would have pushed myself when I had the job interview. I knew I needed a job not only for myself but for her. She's made me more responsible and I've done better in my exams and I've worked at my English. I was really pleased when I got the job. You go to the tech on day release, take an exam every year and by the end of the third year you should be a qualified accounting technician. From there, if you want to, you can go on to be an accountant. I'll have to see how it goes and after about three years, I'll see if I feel like doing any more.

When I wrote out the application form and it said did I have any experience, I just adapted it. I put I had been to the grammar school and I got my O levels. I said I was going to tech on a night for my maths A level and I was also taking General and English. I didn't put about Louisa because a lot of people are a bit biased. But at the interview he said, "I couldn't figure out if you were at school or not", so I told him and he said, "And you've managed to do your A levels?" I said, "Yes", and I plugged it that I'd done it while I'd had Louisa and that's what I think went in my favour in a way. If she can manage A levels and a baby she can manage doing this work. He also wanted a personality to fit into the office. As I was picked from about a hundred applicants I think I did quite well.

I told him that my mum, sister and dad were looking

after Louisa – my parents are retired now – so he knew there was someone looking after her. And I had an incentive to work hard because the higher you go, the more exams you pass, and the more money you get. Another thing about being a qualified accountant is that I could always leave and do books at home. By that time she should be at school, and nursery when she's three. My friend said, "Don't you think you'll be shirking your responsibility?" I said, "No, I'll be getting money this way for her." It's better having more money than living in rags. I've always wanted to work in a bank so even if I hadn't have had Louisa it's basically what I'd have gone on to do anyway. If it hadn't have been for her I wouldn't have been taking so many exams. The more you pass the more money you get and you get better qualifications.

I get about £78 net and I think I get some allowances for Louisa. I got £28.30 altogether before from social security when I was seventeen. When I was eighteen I got £33.70. My mum never took any board but now I've got this job I'll have to start paying her. I buy clothes from my family allowance. Now that I've finished my English and don't have a tutor I'll be able to get more. I was also paying for my moped. And I learned to drive – mum and dad paid for my driving lessons and I paid for the driving test. I've always been good at saving. It's never gone through my fingers. My sister used to borrow from me and I used to charge her interest. My brother said that I would make a good banker. I know I'm better off at home at the moment. If I had a place of my own I'd have to bring Louisa around here. I would also be lonely. One day I will have my own place, but not until I've got some money behind me.'

4
PREGNANCY AND BIRTH

Pregnancy

The pregnancy test is positive. Girls who secretly knew that they wanted a baby, or who may have been trying to have one, feel pleased and excited. Others have a mixture of feelings which tend to become more optimistic as time goes on, but at the initial discovery, pregnancy may seem like a disaster. As we have seen, it is not uncommon for girls to have great difficulty telling their parents or anyone about it, and they may delay this revelation for many months or even right up to when they are going into labour. Some do not realise that they are pregnant at all, like Lorraine, who had never even started her periods. Parents become increasingly worried as they see their daughters putting on weight, and make suggestions about diets, and in Joanne's case, fear they have developed a thyroid condition. Often girls in this situation are not only skilful in concealing their pregnancy through the loose style of clothes they wear, but remain physically small – that is, until finally the truth is out, and suddenly their pregnancy also seems to expand, as if with relief that it can at last be public.

Not surprisingly then, pregnant teenagers are more likely to delay going to the doctor, and in one study,[1] over a quarter had not gone until they were more than three months pregnant. Half of these had not realised that they were pregnant, and others had not wanted to confirm their fears, or didn't see a need to go earlier, or were afraid the doctor might tell their parents. Becoming officially pregnant so late means that many girls do not attend antenatal classes or clinic appointments, they carry on smoking and drinking, and probably eating food that is not particularly healthy. It is during the first few months in particular that these sorts of activities can affect the developing foetus, producing babies that may be premature, and with a low birth weight. A significant number of the mothers I spoke to had had babies who were between four and eleven weeks premature. Medical evidence also shows that however good the care, younger mothers (under fifteen-year-olds) have an increased risk of premature labour.

In the normal way, a pregnant woman would go for regular check-ups either with her doctor or with the antenatal clinic, the first visit being around the eighth to twelfth week. Here a check is kept on weight; blood and urine tests are carried out; and relevant medical history is noted. These checks are very important because they can show, for instance, if there are likely to be any difficulties with the birth which may make a Caesarean section necessary. The blood tests also show up certain abnormalities, such as spina bifida and Downs Syndrome (mongolism). If these can be detected early enough, then women can decide whether or not to continue the pregnancy. This involves a special test (amniocentisis) which has to be done between sixteen and eighteen weeks. Debbie, who has a daughter with spina bifida, had not had this test and only discovered her baby's condition when she was nearly eight months pregnant. One study[2] showed that about half of teenage mothers did not go to the antenatal clinic until the third or fourth month, almost one in five had waited until the fifth month of pregnancy, and a few did not go at all. These later attenders tended to be women who were younger, single, and working class.

For girls who had delayed making their pregnancy

public, at the time it seemed impossible to tell anyone, but afterwards they all wished that they had. Part of this was because they now felt they had missed being pregnant, missed the recognition and attention this involves, and simply the enjoyment it can bring. Lisa, who didn't tell anyone until she was about eight months pregnant said:

> You should tell people straightaway that you're pregnant, because that is one thing I regret, not being able to enjoy my pregnancy properly. I mean I couldn't have, what with being sick and everything, but still I would have liked to tell everyone that I was pregnant. Just being able to enjoy it more instead of being scared and worrying when people were going to find out. It's going to happen, so you might as well tell them. It's easier said than done, but I would if I could go back over it again.

Antenatal classes can be extremely helpful in explaining aspects of pregnancy, labour and birth; and in providing useful exercises and advice, and practice in baby care; and information on the type of pain relief available, what to ask for, and when. These classes are usually run by local midwives, health visitors, or within the local health centre, or by the National Childbirth Trust. They are unpopular with teenage mothers, however, either because they don't see the importance of going, or sometimes because they have been deterred by their experiences at classes where the other mothers are older and married. This had happened to Shirley: 'I went along to one and I felt so different. It was like people were looking at me and guessing my age and looking to see if I had a ring on my finger. I never went back after that.'

This had also been Marie's experience, even though she had got married when she was four months pregnant:

> I was the youngest one there. They'd all had kids before. I thought it would make a difference being a Mrs but it

didn't. I didn't talk to anyone there. They didn't talk to me. They made me feel like a dirty slag and serve me right for getting pregnant. I suppose I was paranoid. Plus I felt guilty at getting pregnant. I wondered if anybody knew I'd got pregnant before I was married. I was only sixteen, just come out of school, straight into antenatal classes.

Antenatal classes could be more sensitive to their younger members, and fortunately some classes do exist specifically geared towards this age group. At a hospital in Manchester, the midwives had just started a Teenage Parent Club. From a local survey they found that many girls of this age were very frightened in labour, which made it worse, and that they had little idea about coping with a tiny baby. But they were very reluctant to attend antenatal classes and so this club had been set up in response to this. Here the girls meet the hospital staff and get used to the relevant delivery rooms and wards; they learn about the changes to expect in their bodies; are advised on appropriate food and clothes; and practise childcare. They are told about maternity grants and other benefits, the possibility of having a social worker, and lots of other useful information.

Sadly, pregnant girls were not yet flocking to this club, even after a launch day at the civic centre, and radio advertising. More community midwives are needed to persuade girls to come, but the most effective way at present is word of mouth. The initial publicity had, however, encouraged some pregnant girls along, including Sara, who had started coming when she was twenty-four weeks pregnant, and now had three-and-a-half weeks left to go. On the day I was there, she had brought along two of her friends who were in a much earlier stage of pregnancy.

If you go to the normal parents' class you get – Oh yeah

– another one, doesn't know a lot, just got pregnant for the fun of it, but the midwives, Ros and Maureen, they treat you different. I've learnt a lot of things – how to bath a baby, feed a baby, it sounds dead simple but when you get that baby in your hands you're shaking. Especially because mine was crying – I think the one I bathed was only a day-and-a-half old, so it was a bit scary. We did pain relief, and I did all my exercises, had films, talks, books that give me advice and everything, dead good they are. And that's why I got my two friends to come. I used to work with them before I finished at the same YTS scheme. I talked them into it because at first they were scared, one because they thought they'd get docked for it – but they said we could have half a day off for it and not get docked – and also because they thought Ros and Maureen were going to be looking down on them, 'Oh, you're only young girls', things like that. Like the midwife who came to see me said, 'Ooh, you're only seventeen', and I looked at her – how old do you have to be to have a baby – forty or something? It's happened and you can't condemn me for it. And when you go to your antenatal clinic, they just look at you and look at your finger to see if you've got a ring on, and then give you a dirty look, and I think, Oh, get lost.

It also gave Sara a sympathetic outlet when she was feeling low:

If I'm down or arguing with one of the family, because I've been ratty through not being well, then Pat the physiotherapist, I have a talk with her and she talks to me and it helps me to talk to somebody else. Like at home I couldn't talk to my mum about it, and I couldn't talk to my boyfriend about it. The one person I could talk to was Pat and she was great.

Some teenage mothers get on fine at the usual antenatal classes, but others, like Sara and her friends, obviously do find it much more helpful to go somewhere with people in a similar situation, so they can share experiences and gain a sense of friendship and solidarity. It can become a pleasant social occasion rather than a chore. Teenage antenatal classes exist in quite a few hospitals now, but there are not nearly enough.

One aspect that not all antenatal classes give enough attention to is the special needs of black mothers, and those from other ethnic groups whose family patterns, food and diets may be different. And according to one study of young black mothers, they are often deterred from attending clinics and classes because of judgemental and discriminatory treatment by hospital and community staff.[3]

If a young woman is feeling fit and healthy, it is very tempting to skip the effort of going to the clinic, having to make an appointment long in advance, and then waiting in long queues, but it is extremely important to have regular check-ups for the sake of both your health and that of your baby.

Experiences of being pregnant

Once the early shock is over, if girls have come to terms with being pregnant, there are a lot of enjoyable things about it, as many girls have found. In common with a lot of other mothers-to-be, they find they are blooming with good health, they get a lot of extra care and attention, and they feel special:

> I loved being pregnant. I am a small and thin person and being fat was great!   (Debbie, pregnant at sixteen)

> My pregnancy was really good. I felt sickly occasionally but I felt really happy throughout my pregnancy. I used

to be quite shy but since I found out I was pregnant I felt very confident in myself. I suppose I was proud of myself. I found my changing body very comical at times. It just looked so out of proportion and we had a few giggles about it. (Lucy, pregnant at sixteen)

Apart from being sick and having to keep going to the loo I loved being pregnant. It felt so special carrying this little person inside me. It was so wonderful every time she kicked although towards the end I got terrible backache and I was so tired all the time. (Wendy, pregnant at sixteen)

I must admit I did like being pregnant. I myself felt special. I used to love it when he kicked me and enjoyed just sitting and feeling the bulge. I felt at peace.
(Marie, pregnant at sixteen)

I felt wonderful, healthy, excited and very feminine carrying the baby. I didn't care about my body changing shape. I thought it looked lovely. (Noreen, pregnant at fourteen)

I felt my lump quite comforting, soothing. I liked just lying there after the antenatal classes, holding my lump and feeling the baby move gently. (Denise, pregnant at seventeen)

Everyone has a different experience of pregnancy, and some are troubled by less pleasurable effects like backache, morning sickness, fainting, and high blood pressure, as well as other physical or emotional changes:

I was happy that I was having my own baby but sometimes I used to cry for nothing and I was easily upset. I was ever so surprised when my belly started blowing up, it always felt so hard, and it was great to feel my baby moving about inside. I couldn't walk until he was born,

I had very high blood pressure and I used to get very bad swollen ankles. Where I was stretching I used to itch all over and I used to get very upset.　(Bridget, pregnant at thirteen)

I had morning sickness all the way through my pregnancy. I looked awful and felt awful most of the time.
(Lisa, pregnant at sixteen)

Growing large and pregnant conflicts with the pressure on women to look slim and beautiful. Expecting a baby is obviously a special state of 'fatness' which can be enjoyed. As Debbie, observed, she could eat and eat and not worry about getting fat. And also there can be something especially beautiful about a pregnant body that many men and women appreciate. But some of these young mothers did not like losing their figures, and also found the stretch marks particularly hard to deal with. Stretch marks are a normal reaction to the skin stretching to accommodate the growing baby, and fade away in time. Some people have them more conspicuously than others, and if you are not expecting this, and even if you are, it can be a very upsetting aspect of pregnancy, as several mothers had found:

The thing I hated most about my pregnancy was the hot weather and my body changing. I had quite a nice figure before but now along with the stretch marks, I hate my body.　(Elaine, pregnant at fifteen)

For Anna, pregnant at eighteen, her stretch marks had had quite a devastating effect on her by the time she was eight months pregnant:

Some were up to an inch wide and ten or eleven inches long. These have covered my thighs, my calves, my belly, my backside and my breasts. 'They'll fade,' people say. I know they will, but only from purple to pink or

95

silver. They will always be there. At the moment I look as if someone has slashed wildly at me with a knife. If this had been the case I may possibly have been offered some cosmetic surgery, but this won't happen because it's a natural part of pregnancy. However natural it is, it still has the effect of making me cry when I catch sight of myself, and nurses have visibly cringed upon seeing them. As well as being unsightly, they have also been very painful, resulting in my not being able to wear tights, etc. and often not being able to touch them to rub various oils and ointments on them to ease the pain. This may all sound very trivial but it has the effect of making me almost hate my body to the extent that I feel ashamed to let John see me naked. There was also a stage where I deeply resented the foetus, although now I think I have killed this feeling. Being pregnant is hard work, no one told me that. I didn't suffer from morning sickness but I've become an insomniac over the months and had the good fortune (or so they tell me) to have a healthy foetus that started kicking me at thirteen weeks.

Two months after having her son, Anna still had her stretch marks:

People tell me they'll fade and that I shouldn't worry about them, or that I shouldn't bother about things like that when I've got a baby, but I can't help it. It's made me lose a lot of self-confidence in myself.

Amongst the girls I talked to, experiences of pregnancy were on the whole mixed. There was a lot of enjoyment to be had, but this was tempered by the anxieties and fears that many had felt during earlier stages, when girls were worrying about parents' reactions, or trying to conceal the pregnancy. Not always knowing what to expect makes some of the physical and emotional changes associated with pregnancy harder to deal with – things like feeling more vulnerable, being easily upset, and crying a lot, are easier to take if you know this is a normal, if disturbing, aspect of pregnancy. If girls have support from their family and from their boyfriends, this can make an enormous difference to this experience, but if they are on their own, it can be very tough.

Birth

The sort of birth you have cannot easily be predicted. Everyone is different, and although obviously some birth complications can be foreseen, such as if the baby is in an unusual position, or if the mother is particularly small and slim, in general, every expectant mother goes into labour hoping for the best, hoping that she'll be the one to have a quick and easy time. However, the labour accompanying the birth of a first baby is often quite long and can be difficult, and this is true whatever the age of the mother. Learning about both pregnancy and birth at antenatal classes can be a great help. The fear that many teenage mothers have when they are wheeled into the delivery room makes the experience more painful and terrifying than it need be.

The length of labour of the mothers in this book ranged from about five hours to twenty-six hours. Although a few had had quick and relatively painless births, many had found it a very painful experience. Some knew about the various methods of pain relief available, but others had no idea at all, and this made them feel even less in control of what was happening to them. The three basic methods are gas and air, which many had used, some so enthusiastically that they ended up either very sleepy, or as one said, 'as high as a kite'. Then there are pethidine injections, which are also quite commonly given to lessen the pain. The strongest method is the epidural, which is a form of local anaesthetic, injected in the base of the spine, which numbs the body from the waist down. This gives complete pain relief and is helpful for women having a long labour or who are getting very distressed, but it has disadvantages in that it obviously makes women feel quite passive and helpless. It also means that they cannot feel the contractions, so the midwife has to tell them when to push, which can take longer.

Sometimes there can be complications, and forceps have to be used to pull the baby out, or other more serious problems arise and a Caesarean section is performed. When the baby is born, sometimes the vaginal entrance will not stretch enough for its head to pass through. In this case a local anaesthetic is used and a little cut made in the perineum. This is called an episiotomy. After the baby is born, the cut is stitched up and heals. It is quite a normal procedure, and for two mothers who had quite easy births, having these stitches had been the worst thing about it.

Every experience of childbirth is different, so the accounts by teenage mothers that follow illustrate just a few of these. Some had relatively easy births, others were very painful and often traumatic. Jane had a short and fairly easy time, as did Folasade, who had told no one but her boyfriend that she was pregnant:

My pregnancy was lovely. I was skinny but I'd never been so healthy in my life. And I had a two-hour labour. No stitches. I just had him. They left me alone because they thought I had hours to go. They hadn't bothered to check my cervix. With a first baby you're a long time, especially with my build. But I started labour and just had him in the room. The nurses happened to come in. I was sitting up and I said, 'I feel a bit funny'. I just looked down and his hair was sticking out. They said, 'Don't panic. Stay there. Don't move!' It was painful and the more painful it became the nearer I knew I was getting.

So I thought, this is so bad something's happening. Then it started to slow down, and I was sick. I had nothing else to do, so I just started pushing. That hurt, but it wasn't horrible pain. So when they came back they said, 'Push', and out he came. That was two hours of pain, the whole thing might have been a little longer. But I got to hospital by half-past eight in the morning and by eleven o'clock I'd had him. I was relaxed and I wasn't worried or scared.   (Jane)

As soon as I'd woken up, I started to get strange pains in my stomach. I'm quite a lazy person so I ignored them. I carried on. Everyone was wandering around the house getting everything ready for my uncle who had come over from Nigeria. I got dressed and they got slightly worse. About eight o'clock they were getting very bad so I went to bed. I told everyone I wasn't well. Then my sister came in. We share a room. By that time they were bad, so I told her I thought I was having a miscarriage. She didn't even know I was pregnant. She raced to the bathroom and got a bowl of water and a towel. I said I didn't need it. So she said, 'Shall I tell Mummy?' I said, 'No'. I said I was thirsty so she went to get me a drink.

I had to get up because when I walked I found it was easier. I walked into the bathroom and by then labour had started. So I told her, 'Go and get Mum.' Our house is only a flat, it's not very long, and from the time it took my sister to leave me, go to the kitchen and tell my mum and bring her back, the baby was in my arms. I was standing up, so I suppose that helped. So the baby was already out. I had one leg up on the bath and I had the baby. It was weird because as soon as she came out I started to wash her. You know the white stuff they have on them, I thought – Oh, you're a bit dirty aren't you, so

99

I started washing her.

My mum came in and said, 'What is this?' You can imagine what I said. I said, 'Oh, that's a baby.' The umbilical cord and the afterbirth were still inside me, so she began to yank this baby and I said , 'Excuse me, I've still got a bit inside me.' Thinking about it now, it's funny. But it was very uncomfortable at the time. She took me into my brother's room, he hadn't come back yet. She stripped the bed and lay me on the bed. All the films you see, they never show the mother having the afterbirth. I didn't know you had to deliver that as well. Then Mum started saying, 'Push.' I said, 'Push what?' She didn't tell me what I was doing, so all right, I pushed, and I gave birth to the afterbirth and thought, Oh, that's why she wanted me to push. It was all very innocent. I didn't really know what was going on after I'd had the baby. Mum just wrapped her up, rang the ambulance, and I was taken to hospital.   (Folasade)

I had a show about 11.30 a.m. I was pleased as I was already a week-and-a-half overdue. I thought it wasn't worth just sitting around waiting for something to happen and I had already arranged to go to my friend's house so I went out. I didn't really feel a thing until about 5.30 p.m. when I began to feel a sort of tightening of the stomach, not a pain. So my friend rang the hospital so that they were ready for me. They told me not to bother to go in until the contractions became regular. I went home from my friend's about 6.30 p.m. Not a lot was happening and I was really tired so I decided to go to bed. My mum got home from work about 10.30 p.m. and asked if I was all right, but I told her that I thought it was a false alarm.

I woke up about 12.30 that night, and I really did know I was in labour by this time. I was really shaking.

I called my mum and dad and asked if they could take me to the hospital. I got there and they asked me why I didn't get there sooner. I just said I was asleep. By this time the pain was really bad. I think the worst thing was that I couldn't stop shaking. I wasn't really afraid, I just held onto my Mum's hand. About 2.30 a.m. I asked if they could give me something for the pain. They gave me a pethidine injection which just made me feel a bit sleepy. I had Stuart about 3.55 a.m. which I'm told wasn't bad for my first child. I think I was expecting it all to be much worse, but I enjoyed it and could honestly say that it was one of the best days of my life. (Shirley)

I'd been given a date for the baby to arrive but that came and went, but then I woke up in the early hours of the following Friday. I often used to get stomach-ache if I hadn't had enough to eat so when I woke up with a pain I thought maybe I was hungry again, but because the baby was due any day I thought it best to tell my mum. She was quite calm and told me to get a watch and try and time how far apart the pains were. So I sat in bed with a slice of bread and jam in one hand and a watch in the other, trying to time the pains. They didn't hurt exactly, it was more of a niggly pain but I worked it out to about once every four minutes or so and my mum said we'd better ring the hospital. The hospital said I'd better go in and sent an ambulance round for me. It's funny, but as me, my mum and dad, all piled into the back of the ambulance, I remember thinking it was a shame it was so early in the morning and there wasn't anyone around to see me go.

At the hospital I was put into a side room and a nurse came and examined me. It was about six in the morning and the nurse thought I would have the baby by about twelve o'clock. I'd heard stories of women being in labour for twelve or fifteen hours with their first child so I was quite pleased. The nurse was wrong. The doctors had already decided I should have an epidural for the birth. The baby was quite big for me because I was so small. I didn't know what an epidural was, but I knew I wouldn't have any pain so it was okay by me. I had the epidural injection in the base of my spine and then I was all rigged up to a machine so the nurses could monitor the baby's movements. The epidural numbs you from the waist down so I couldn't feel any of the contractions.

By now I think mum and dad had gone home but they'd rang Ian and he'd come straight to the hospital and sat with me. I felt okay, I had no pains, except for a belt around my waist. It was attached to the monitor so the nurses could see what was happening to the baby and every time I had a contraction my stomach went rock hard so the belt dug into me. It was quite painful, especially as the time went on and the contractions were coming closer together. But the nurse couldn't move it and I had to put up with it. I did make a bit of fuss about it and the nurse told me to stop moaning. Then unfortunately for me, the nurses forgot to top up the epidural injection and the pain killer started to wear off. I could feel every contraction and it was agony. The nurses topped it up again as soon as they realised but it took time to go through and have any effect so I had about twenty minutes of real labour pains. Up until then I still wasn't too worried, but I think then it started to dawn on me that this wasn't going to be much fun and I felt a bit scared. I didn't know what to expect and no-one had really told me. Perhaps they didn't want to scare me and thought it better not to say too much, but I wish they had said something. The epidural was working and I couldn't feel any real pain apart from the belt and I was lying there watching the monitor shoot up and down as the baby moved around.

Then suddenly a doctor walked in all dressed up in his green gown and a face mask and said, 'Hello, this is it then,' and a nurse took my ankles and shoved them into some stirrups and covered me up in all this green cloth. In the doorway there were about six or seven young student doctors all in their white coats smiling at me, and the nurses were milling around and talking. I wondered what the hell was going on and I suddenly felt absolutely terrified. I don't remember anyone of them saying anything to me. They knew what they were doing, but I didn't. I wanted my mum or Ian, but my mum was at home and Ian had been told to go into the waiting room. I screamed and cried all the way through the birth. I had a nurse either side of me telling me to push, but I couldn't push. I was numb from the waist down and couldn't feel anything. In the end the doctor had to cut me and use forceps to drag the baby out. They took the baby and I remember asking if it was okay and did I have a boy or a girl. I'd always wanted a little girl, but one of the students at the door told me I had a beautiful little boy and he was fine. I was so relieved it was all over and my baby was alright and I held him for the first time. He was gorgeous.   (Mary)

Sometimes when it is not possible to have a normal birth, a Caesarean section is performed. This may be because the mother's pelvis is too small, or because the baby is in an awkward position in the womb or gets in distress. Lesley started haemorrhaging before her baby was due. The speed at which everything then happened made it all seem rather unreal:

I just couldn't get comfortable. The most comfortable position was to stand up. I made the bed and was putting the clothes in the cupboard. I sat down, and then stood

up, and there was blood everywhere. I had two months
to go. At the hospital I got changed and was in the
admittance room and I heard my dad outside saying, 'Do
you want me to sign for anything?' I had this idea they
had booked me in for a Caesarean because I'm small, but
hadn't told me. They took me down to the labour room.
They put monitors on me, and injections in my arms.
They said that's just in case the baby comes early, that's
all they said. And then they got me to sign a form, they
didn't say what it was for. A doctor came and said, 'You'll
probably be having the baby today.' But nobody told
me. And they sent Alan off for his dinner in the hospital canteen and when he came back I'd gone. I just
remember them wheeling me down to this room and
going to sleep. I woke up and I was aching. And he was
sitting there. I said, 'What's happening?' they said,
'You've had a baby.' I said 'What is it?' I thought that
being pregnant had been a dream and I'd woken up. I
had no idea I'd had a baby. I didn't know what the hell
was going on. Everybody kept coming in. I kept going to
sleep and waking up. It was the next afternoon that I first
saw her, she was in an incubator. Tubes and wires
everywhere. She only weighed three pounds.

Lesley's baby daughter was premature, in common with
quite a number of other teenage mothers. She therefore
had to go into Intensive Care, as do other babies who may
have had birth complications or other problems. This may
mean that a mother is left on her own in the ward, while all
the other mothers are sitting there nursing their babies.
This can be a disconcerting and distressing experience, and
some young mothers are not confident enough to ask to see
their babies and may end up feeling as though they have
not really had one. Nickie's baby was eleven weeks premature. She had not even had the support of her mother,

sister, or boyfriend while she gave birth, and the baby had to stay in hospital for several weeks after she returned alone to her bedsit:

I had a little stomach-ache and I thought it was something I'd eaten. It didn't occur to me that I was in labour because it was too early. But the thing I hated most was that there was nobody there. All these other women in labour, other girls had a mum or a sister there. I had nobody. I phoned my sister and said, 'I'm in labour', but she said, 'I'm working tomorrow and I can't come.' I was really frightened. People told me it is like a period pain, and to start with it was very like a period pain. And then later I had an epidural because the pain was so bad. And there was nobody there. I keep thinking to myself that if somebody had been there I would have managed, but there wasn't. It lasted twenty-two hours. I've never felt anything like that. She came out and they lay her on my stomach. They let me hold her for a few minutes and then they took her away upstairs to Special Care.

I saw her at six the following evening. I kept saying, 'Can I see her?' 'No, we're busy, I'll get someone to take you up in a minute.' I finally got upstairs and she had all these tubes attached to her, it was horrible. She looked so tiny. I'd seen premature babies but never a baby that small. She couldn't breathe properly, I thought she was going to die. After all the tubes had gone my family came to see her, before that they didn't want to come and see her. It was embarrassing because the nurses kept saying, 'Where's the baby's father? Where's your mum?'

I'll never forget being in hospital. I was in a ward with four beds and all these women had their babies beside them and I didn't. That really did hurt. This woman came round to take pictures. They look at you and they assume, if the baby's not there, your baby must have died. They just ignore you as if you're not there. Finally I said, 'She's in Special Care, she's not dead!' It was a long while before I could even change her nappy, and putting clothes on, you had to disconnect all the wires, put the clothes on and put them all back.

After having a baby, the usual feelings are relief, joy, tiredness, and overwhelming love for the tiny baby. Teenage mothers are no different from any other mothers in this respect. But some get very depressed. Studies have shown evidence that teenagers may be particularly susceptible to depression after childbirth.[4] This may be associated with financial or housing problems, loneliness, problems with relationships, or difficulties coping with the responsibility of having a tiny baby. A few of the mothers talking here had also experienced quite severe postnatal depression and detachment from their babies. Joanne and Diane were two of these. Joanne had delayed telling anyone until four days before she went into labour. She had a difficult labour as, having no details, the curvature of her spine was not detected. She had very high blood pressure, and was given two epidurals that didn't work. At one point, her sister, who was there with her, was almost asked to choose between her and the baby. Her daughter was taken away to Special Care, and she, like Nickie, hated seeing fathers come in looking pleased while she sat alone on her bed, waiting for her mother.

I had terrible postnatal depression. I used to just sit and cry. Up until she was about four months old. If anybody said anything to upset me I'd just burst out crying. That wasn't like me. At the slightest mention of her father's name I got upset, and even when people said isn't she a gorgeous little baby. She cried when she first came home. I used to get so cross with her. I think if Mum hadn't been here I'd have done something to her. I thought it annoyed Dad, and we'd get kicked out.

The first six weeks I didn't want to know. She wasn't mine, nothing to do with me. It took me quite a long time to get over it. I think I was so detached when I first had her because of the mental blockage, and the labour, and the birth was so messy and horrible. In a way I blamed her for it, and to start with I think I hated her. I thought she was going to pin me down and that would be it. I'd been so used to my freedom. The mental blockage just carried on. It wasn't until she was really ill that I realised she was mine and I loved her more than anything. From then on I just didn't look back. She's mine and that was it.

The birth of Diane's son was 'the worst experience of my life'. She found it very painful indeed. And despite having had a good, healthy pregnancy, she had already started getting depressed:

In the last month I got depressed. Suddenly I felt detached from the baby. All through the pregnancy I felt special, then suddenly all my friends didn't want to know me, only one friend, Karen, and she made me feel worse, as she was so glamourous and I was sitting there all fat.

When he was born I felt detached. I heard him cry immediately and the doctor say it's a boy, but I didn't feel part of it. He was put in my arms and immediately he stopped crying but it was so strange I didn't feel anything. In the early weeks after I had him I suffered from postnatal depression. I felt as if the slightest thing, even feeding the baby, was too much. I was extremely tired and the night feeds really got me down. I couldn't feel anything for him and sometimes even resented him. I'd feed him and clothe him but not because I loved him. I had to, to keep him alive. It affects you funny. One

107

minute I was happy and the next I was depressed. I was crying all the time. My mum got fed up with it. I'd read all about it but when you've actually got it, it's horrible. Nobody talked about it in the classes, only the birth and the pregnancy, not about the baby afterwards, or how you will feel. I went through a long period of thinking of having him adopted. Now I am very ashamed of the way I felt but at the time my feelings were very strong. As time went on these feelings wore off. Now I love him very much, he is a little person in his own right. Now I feel like any other mother. I love him, I play with him, I feel normal. I rush round to the health visitor if something is wrong with him. I'd never do that before. When I had depression I went to a self-help group. I still attend as I do get days when I feel depressed. I'm beginning to cope and adjust gradually. I've been depressed before, at not having a job I suppose. Even now though, I still get depressed.

Some teenage mothers complain bitterly about the attitudes and treatment they receive in antenatal clinics and classes and in hospital, which are sometimes patronising and even rude. They have been treated as people who did not know what they were doing, have made some terrible mistake and are wasting their lives. They are quite rightly upset and offended as they have usually made their own decisions and are going through with them. Doreen, a nineteen-year-old mother of three young children, felt strongly about this after her experiences, and correctly points out that it was her own choice to have her children, and she should be given the same respect as any older mother:

When I went to the antenatal clinic for my very first check-up, this elderly doctor burst through the door, looked at me and said, 'You shouldn't be having this baby, you should be giving it away to somebody less fortunate.' I felt upset because I wanted the baby.

I saw this TV programme, about girls of fifteen who had had abortions, and they said the nurses made them feel they shouldn't be having abortions, they should keep the baby. Yet when I was having my baby they made me feel as though I shouldn't be having it. That I should have had an abortion or given it away. You can't win.

I was fifteen, and the nurses treated me as though I shouldn't have been there. They stuck me in a ward with four older women who were married. They spoke to them nicely, but if I asked them for anything it was as though they couldn't be bothered. And the other patients didn't know whether to speak to me or not. I felt really out of place.

A year later when I had Katie and I was married, I didn't want to go to hospital in case I got the same treatment, but they were totally different. Just because I had a wedding ring on. They talked to me, I couldn't understand the difference. It was all the same nurses and midwives. They remembered me from the previous year too.

They seem to think that teenage mothers can't look after children properly. If I had felt that I couldn't cope with him, I probably would have had him adopted, or had an abortion, but it was my choice to have him.

5
SUBSTITUTE HOMES

If you are young and pregnant but your family is unwilling or unable to accommodate you and a baby, and you don't have a boyfriend or husband to look after you, your only alternatives may be a Mother and Baby Home, or less frequently, some fostering arrangement. Traditionally, Mother and Baby Homes were religious-based, charity-run institutions that took in girls who had 'fallen', and cared for them during their pregnancy and for some time afterwards. Parents put their daughters in there to hide them away from the public eye until the baby was born and adopted. This attitude has changed somewhat over the years and there are now fewer homes than there used to be. Those that still exist continue to be quite well-subscribed. They are usually open to girls from around the age of fourteen upwards. Sometimes girls are there because they are very young or they are homeless, sometimes it is because their parents cannot cope at home with the responsibility for them and a newborn baby, and in other cases a home takes in and assesses girls whose ability to look after their baby is in question. The girls and women who go there are not necessarily teenagers, some may be in their twenties and thirties. Finding such a home is usually done through social workers or pregnancy counselling agencies.

Some homes are still religious and dependent on the church, some are run by local authorities, and others are a combination of both. The Catholic Church, for instance, runs a network of such homes called Life Houses as part of its constant effort to persuade pregnant girls not to have abortions. The Church of England is also responsible for some homes, but unmarried mothers have never been a very popular cause for charity funding, and therefore these often depend mainly on local funding.

A few of the teenage mothers in this book had been in such a home. Sheila stayed in one until her daughter was born and adopted; Denise left London to live in the West Country on her own, and organised a place in one for herself and her eight-week-old baby; and Lisa went into one when she was about six months pregnant.

Another kind of Mother and Baby Home looks after girls who, in addition to being pregnant, have particular social or medical problems. One of these is run in a large old house in its own grounds in North London which has been used as a private Mother and Baby Home since the late 1920s. It is a Church of England Home, now funded mainly by local boroughs and minimally by church donations. It caters for up to fifteen girls and babies, from fourteen years old upwards. In its earlier days, pregnant girls would come there because they were homeless, they would stay six weeks before and after the birth and their babies were almost invariably adopted. This pattern has been changing; there is a tendency now for girls to keep their babies, and over the last year or so girls have been sent there for a variety of other reasons, but essentially so that they can be assessed on their ability to care for their child.

Girls may be there simply because they are young and things are not working out at home or with their boyfriends, or they may be designated as 'ESN' (educationally sub-normal), or have had previous children that they have lost through negligence or ignorance. A significant number have been brought up in children's homes themselves. It is the staff's role to give an assessment on the girl and her basic care of the baby and her anticipation of its needs.

It also gives girls some breathing space from all their other problems. The average stay is five to six months, but sometimes it may be as much as a year.

It is the babies who come first here, and the mother a close second. As well as being taught the basic techniques of childcare, some girls may also need to learn how to give and take love, if they have come from environments in which they experienced very little love and affection. There are very few rules, girls can get up and go to bed when they like, and have visitors up to ten o'clock at night. The main concern is getting a good routine with the baby. All the girls have social workers, or probation officers, or welfare officers. The present superintendent estimated at this time that about half of all girls coming there had never really had any home life, or had been in care, and believed that this cycle would repeat itself: 'as high as 85 per cent of these babies, it's going to happen to them. And then again I think it is escapism for some of them to get pregnant where there's so much unemployment, it's something of their own to be proud about. So I think it is a circle.'

It is possible that Barbara, a sixteen-year-old West Indian girl living in the Home with her two-week-old baby may get trapped in that circle. She, together with her brother and sister, had been in care – a children's home on the south coast – from the age of four until ten years old. Unlike the mothers of some of the other children, her mother came to see them quite a lot, and she remembers it not being so bad – 'once you get used to it, it's just like your home'. When she got pregnant her social worker booked her into here, as there was not much space at her home and Barbara agreed that it wasn't right that her mother should have her back with a baby as well. She had already left home several times to stay with her boyfriend. As she was still at school, she had been assigned a tutor but this had stopped as they did not get on. Although she was looking forward to leaving the home, she felt she wasn't ready to go quite yet, and her baby son had been harder to cope with than she'd expected.

After I get out of here, I'll just have my flat and I'll continue. It's not as if everything's done for you here. You have to look after your baby yourself here, so it's the same when you leave. I'm not saying it's easy. He's a hard job. It's all right here. When I first came I couldn't stand it. I never used to stay here more than two days. They used to have to drag me back. But when you get used to it, it's quite an all right place.

For every girl they take in there are many more who end up in bed and breakfast where they are more likely to suffer from living alone in unsuitable accommodation. Often it is girls from already deprived backgrounds who end up in such circumstances, and who are less able to cope on their own. After staying here, most girls, apart from the very young ones, go off to their own flats. A few go to a kind of 'halfway house', of which there should be many more, which usually consists of four or five small flatlets which girls either share or occupy on their own. They look after themselves, but there is always someone responsible around if they have any problems. Although most girls can't wait to leave the home for their own place to do their own thing, some always come back to show what they've achieved, or to say it wasn't so bad in the home after all.

LISA

Lisa is eighteen and now lives on the nineteenth floor of a block of London flats with her nine-month-old daughter. Her Grenadan boyfriend, the baby's father, lives there too, and gives her a substantial amount of his wages from his clerical job. He is very helpful financially, but does not help Lisa with much else.

She was sixteen and doing some O-level retakes at further education college when she became pregnant. The year before she had missed some exams because her mother had chucked her out of the house for coming in too late at night. She returned home, but she and her mother did not get on very well. Her parents had divorced when she was fourteen, her father had been in and out of prison, was often alcoholic, and had occasionally beaten up her mother. After her divorce her mother suffered a virtual nervous breakdown and Lisa had to look after her and her sisters for a while.

Lisa kept putting off telling her mother she was pregnant. 'I know it was silly really, she'd already thrown me out so she couldn't do much worse really.' She put it off because Christmas was coming up, and then Tony her boyfriend wanted to take her to Paris and she knew if she revealed her pregnancy she wouldn't be allowed to go, so she said nothing. 'Then March came and I thought I can't tell her now, I'm too far gone, she'll go mad.' But her mother had already begun to suspect and sat her down and asked her. She was about twenty-four weeks pregnant by this time.

She had not told Tony either, because she knew he'd want her to have an abortion, and she would have refused, and this would have split them up. She agreed to have an adoption to keep the peace with her mother. Lisa always knew she did not really want her baby adopted, and before she was even born had decided against it. Her father had to be told; Tony was terrified of this joint meeting but it went all right. Lisa was always his favourite and he seemed favourably impressed that Tony had stayed around. Lisa had given him the choice of staying with her, or going off, but she insisted he decide then as she didn't want him leaving in the middle of it all. He chose to stay, although it hasn't always worked out well.

114

Her mother thought it was better for her not to be at home as there was not much space, so the following week they saw the social worker and it was arranged that she go to a house run by the Catholic anti-abortion organisation LIFE. This was chosen more because it was available rather than for religious reasons.

'Two weeks later I was ready to go to a place I didn't know, and where I knew no one. I was very upset and scared. When I arrived the housemother showed me around. There were five bedrooms, one for each girl. We shared the toilets, bathroom, living room and kitchen. It was a lovely big house with a big garden out the back. I was told the rules, there were not that many and most were sensible. No smoking upstairs, no pets, no visitors, and there was a cleaning rota. The housemother didn't live with us, she lived down the road.

That afternoon I sat in my room and unpacked my things. I also cried a lot. At the time there were only three other girls in the house. It felt a bit lonely, the first night I was crying upstairs because all my family came, and me and my sister are really close and it was upsetting to leave her. Then a girl came upstairs and said, "Oh don't be silly, have a cry on my shoulder," and she helped me to settle down. Then she said "Come on downstairs, *Eastenders* is on," so we went down and then I was all right.

Over the next two months I spent my time between staying at my boyfriend's house at weekends and the LIFE house on weekdays. The place was a bit religious but they didn't kind of drum it into you, they used to go on about church a bit. But some of the rules, about not having visitors, meant that all my visitors that came from London had to walk round town. But I used to bring them in anyway, and I used to let them out the back door if the housemother came in.

Most of the girls in there were nice. They were all different ages. After a while it was nice being so far away from home, no one to moan at me. I got used to doing what I wanted to do. It was luxury, lovely. We had to cook our own meals because the housemother wasn't living in; we used to do everything for ourselves. One day I'd cook something and the next day another girl would. We used to have some fun with that.

After I had the baby I stayed seven days in the hospital and then returned to the house. They all thought she was gorgeous and they were all making a big fuss. And making a fuss of me because they knew that my stitches had burst. And like we used to bath the babies by the fire, even though it was mid-July. You should've seen us. I'd taken her back with a woolly suit, mitts, hat, booties, everything, in the middle of July. I was scared she'd get a cold!

They didn't really teach us anything at the house, you just learned for yourself through being there. Once there was a couple of girls who had had their babies and they'd say to you, "Change the baby for us while I run upstairs and get so-and-so" or "Will you feed the baby for me a minute?" or "Can you make up some feeds?" We all helped each other. I knew everything, they couldn't believe it at the hospital. They said, "You've got to have a lesson on how to make up bottles", so I said, "I already know, there's no need" and they said, "We want to make sure". So I made up a couple of bottles for them and they said, "Oh".

After I had the baby, things got bad. Tony let me down time after time. Every time we arranged to come to London he would decide he had other things to do. When I did come he would go out and leave me in, just me, the baby, and four walls. I hated him for that. In January I received my flat, a nice two-bedroomed flat. But things got even worse between me and Tony. We even split up for a while. I took him back because I love him and can't do without him, so now I'm back to square one. I can cope with him and everyday life now. I go to a mother and toddler group nearby. I have a new set of friends and something to look forward to everyday. At the moment I have no plans for the future except I want what's best for my little girl. She comes first before everything.'

Fostering a teenage mother

There is another alternative for young girls who are pregnant and homeless. This is to be fostered. It is an option that is not very often used, either through choice or simply because it is not much publicised. It is obviously different from fostering a small child, because there may be far more potential for personality clashes as young women try to cope with having a baby and having a foster mother. Fostering a teenage mother is therefore something we do not hear a lot about. It came to Noreen's rescue when she was just fifteen, pregnant and living in a Children's Home with little hope of anywhere else to go. For her it had worked well in some ways but not in others, which had mainly to do with the relationship between her and her foster mother after her son Sean was born. In retrospect she had mixed feelings about it. Sadly, at the end of her stay, her promised flat had failed to materialise and she had nowhere to live yet again. She did not want to go to her parents through fear of her father and because she might run into her baby's father. As a last resort, she and her son went back to the Children's Home. Here she felt lonely and depressed, as it seemed as if she'd made no progress and was back in the same vicious circle again.

NOREEN

Noreen is the youngest daughter in a family of four, living in Wales. Tragedy hit them when her youngest brother died of cancer when he was thirteen. It wasn't a very happy family, her father, who worked long hours as an engineer, hit her mother and sometimes the children too, but he never hit Noreen. When she was thirteen, Gerry, who was her sister Rosie's boyfriend at the time, began to take a strong interest in her. She found him nice and easy to talk to, and they soon started seeing each other regularly. They were together for about two-and-a-half years and he is her son Sean's father.

Over a period of about eighteen months, her father hit her mother to such an extent that she went into a Battered Wives Home five times, taking her two daughters with her each time. But she always went back. Noreen and Rosie became very scared seeing their mother so frightened and in pain. When Noreen was fourteen, it happened for the fifth time, and her mother ran out of the house. Her father sent her and Rosie to look for her. They never went back.

They found their mother and went to the Battered Wives Home as usual, this time for six weeks. Rosie was very insecure and a bundle of nerves. Noreen's only reassurance lay in Gerry. Her mother seemed to be coping this time, and they sincerely hoped she wouldn't go back, but she did. Her mother and father saw each other in the street one day and that was it. But Noreen and Rosie would not return and Noreen asked her mother to leave them alone. She told her she was having a relationship with Gerry, but not that they had started sleeping together. Her mother was upset as she didn't approve of Gerry.

At first, Noreen and Rosie stayed at their brother's flat, and then at a friend's, but they weren't very happy there. They went to the Social Services and saw a social worker about finding somewhere else to go. They waited but nothing happened so they made a fuss. The next thing they knew they were on their way to a Children's Home run by nuns about twenty miles away:

118

'It was nice and clean, I had a bath and went to bed. I was so happy. We were so relieved to have got away and to somewhere nice. I used to go home now and again. And I used to see Gerry. Then I stayed with him and got pregnant. That was Christmas. I knew from January but I didn't know who to tell. We never took precautions. I knew one day I would get pregnant. I never worried.

I told Gerry and he was shocked, but he was excited and everything. I wondered what my parents would say. Our social worker came and he said Mum had told him I had a boyfriend. I thought, "Oh No!" But he said, "Don't sleep with him", and all this time I was pregnant. In the end my sister went and got Sister upstairs. I'd been sick. I told Sister. I was the first person in a nun's care to get pregnant. I'm famous! She said that I had to tell my parents. They told my social worker and he told my dad.

Dad said, "If you have an abortion you can come home and we'll forget everything. If you keep the baby I don't want to know." So I said, "I'm keeping the baby." I was prepared to give up my parents, and wanted the baby. I tried to explain that to the Sister. She said, "It's in God's hands." Even my doctor said I ought to have an abortion, because of my age. I was under so much pressure, I couldn't believe it. My doctor had arranged it all and I didn't want to do it. Nobody would help me. In the end I just came out with it to my mum, "I'm having a baby and I'm keeping it." So I lost my parents as well.

Social Services didn't know where to send me to have the baby. I couldn't stay where I was, it's one of the rules. They could only think of another children's home. I didn't want to go. I went to see it but the lady running it said they couldn't take me. Then I said to them, "It's a pity you couldn't find me foster parents", and the social worker said, "What a brilliant idea!"

Sometime later they came back and said, "We think

we've found somebody." It was a couple, with a young son. Pam was a very down-to-earth person and they thought I'd get on well. It was in an upper-class area. I was from a working-class area. He said they had a big swimming pool with the house. I said, "I'm not going to fit in there, but I got excited about it, mainly because of the swimming pool. I needed somewhere to live, I was six months by then. I went to see her and she was lovely.

Pam knew about Rosie, that we'd done everything together and hadn't been split up and that it was hard for me to leave her. We arranged that I'd go for the weekend, but I wouldn't leave my sister. So she said, "Bring her", so she came as well. It was like it was all meant to happen. We got on like a house on fire. Nobody said, "Look, she's only fifteen and she's having a baby." Everyone else had, or that's the impression you get. But they made me feel great, I told them, "I want to live here." So a week later I moved in, and I was there for a year-and-a-half.

It was lovely. Pam prepared me to look after the baby. The whole time I was carrying it, I wasn't worried about the birth. I used to talk to her about it. I used to look at birth books and that, otherwise I wouldn't have had a clue. I'd say, "What's going to happen there?" because I was determined that I was going to have the baby on my own. But I didn't.

My parents wouldn't come and visit me. Mum used to ring me but that was all. I never had their support. I always did everything on my own. I got support from my sister, but I did miss them. They never liked Gerry. Gerry has never seen his own son. When I went to Pam's we still kept contact. Nobody knew this. I still had to talk to him. I spoke to him while Pam went to pick up her son. But it hit me one day, he didn't care or he would have made that effort to come and see me and he didn't. So one day I said, "I've had enough." I haven't seen him since.

I was fifteen-and-a-half when Sean was born. I couldn't have coped when he was first born, with a house or anything. The only thing that made me go into any routine was Pam. She has made a great difference to me, she was wonderful. She's changed my personality altogether. I know if I got a flat tomorrow I could cope, whereas I couldn't have before. She was so helpful. They don't realise how much they've done for me.

But sometimes I felt she took over and I got annoyed about it but didn't like to say. And I didn't want to have to turn to her and say, "Is it all right if I let so-and-so take my son out?" I felt I had to ask her. So until he was about a year old nobody took him out except me.

She used to sometimes say, "You shouldn't do this, they'll take him away." Just to get things through to me. But she didn't need to. I got paranoid about it. I used to think if somebody else took him out they'd take him away. She said it so much I really thought it. I couldn't relax with the baby. Everything I did she watched me. But then when Sean was about fourteen months I couldn't take any more and I'd just do it my way, and I'm glad I did.

Also at times I was overcome by tiredness, really knackered. I couldn't sleep. But the whole point of Pam being there, my being fostered, was if I couldn't cope was for her to take over. But I felt I couldn't give up, for my own sake or the baby's. I wanted to prove I could do it. It used to get to the point where I was completely shattered but I wouldn't ask her to take over and yet she wouldn't offer. She was so good, yet there were so many things she didn't do which I would have thought she would have. It's probably the same vice versa.

There were a lot of little things that I felt were wrong. I think she did as well. And there was her attitude towards the baby. At home she wouldn't bother with him. When she was out she wanted to show him off. I just felt like his sister sometimes. It really got to me. She didn't realise she was doing it. Pam loves children but she doesn't like them when they're mobile, it gets on her nerves. And she said she wanted me to leave – not because of me, any girl who came to her pregnant must leave when the baby's eight or nine months. But of course they hadn't found me anywhere to live. So I was there until Sean was seventeen months, which put a strain on all of us, I think.

The idea was, I was to go to the foster parents, stay there until the baby was born and mobile, and then move to a flat. I just wanted somewhere to live, have the baby, then the two of us to be on our own somewhere. And I still haven't got anywhere.

I think things could have been a lot better at Pam's. If I got fed up with the foster parents there was no one I could turn to really. Although I had them, I didn't have anyone. It's the same here in the home. It does get to the point where you think, "Oh God, is there no one in this world who is going to help me?" It does feel like that sometimes. But I don't know what I'd do if it weren't for Sean. He's the only thing that has kept me going. This is a difficult time now. I've broken down a lot more than I ever have over the last three months. Coming back here. This is where I started off. At Pam's I felt I had achieved something. I felt proud of myself. Then to come back here, everything just goes.'

Since talking to me, she has been given a council house about fifteen miles from her family home, so at last she and Sean can get on with their lives together.

6

HOUSING AND
FINANCIAL SURVIVAL

As a young mother, the options open to you as to where you'll live are probably few. The family home may be one of them, and is where many single girls stay until they are willing and able to move to a place of their own, usually a council house or flat. Sometimes the baby's father, if he is still around, moves in as well. He may even have been living there before the pregnancy. If you are very young, living at home is usually the only choice, unless you go into a Mother and Baby Home, or some other form of 'care', or you can move in with your boyfriend. You are not officially eligible for council housing until you are eighteen,[1] or you may apply for Housing Association accommodation at seventeen.

Living with the family has its advantages and disadvantages. Since many teenage mothers come from larger families who are not well off in terms of money or housing, accommodating another baby may put a strain on space and resources. It can cause stress, resentment and arguments, especially if a boyfriend has moved in as well. Alan hated living at his girlfriend's house, whereas Pete didn't mind sharing one of the two bedrooms in his sixteen-year-old fiancee's parents' house with her and their baby daughter. He paid £20 a week for his keep. Girls on their own with their babies can be more easily absorbed into the family, but there may still be tension and difficulties.

Two young mothers I spoke to were about to be accommodated by their families in a slightly different way. Lorraine and her 21-month-old handicapped son had just received approval from the council to build an extension on the back of the house where they will be able to maintain some autonomy from the rest of the family. Jenny and her five-month-old son lived in quite a large house with her father, stepmother, and two sisters. She had asked for council accommodation without success, so the current plan was to convert the basement into a bedsitter for them.

Unless the local authority decide that the present conditions of housing constitute a risk for the mother and baby, the only way a young mother can get her own place is to be made homeless. To get her three-bedroomed council house, Cathy's mother had to pretend that she was chucking her out because she didn't get on with her stepfather. Fortunately in this rural area there was no shortage of housing, but girls living in inner city areas are more likely to be put in temporary accommodation, consisting of bed and breakfast, or a hotel. This can prove both expensive and not particularly comfortable. Wendy had moved into a flat with her boyfriend when she was pregnant, but it was so cold and damp that the council moved her to a hotel, and later to her council flat. In this hotel Wendy and her baby lived in one tiny room. They got bed and breakfast, and had £19 a week for themselves. As the evening meal cost £2, neither of them ate very much.

Getting rehoused is not always easy or automatic, temporary accommodation is often depressing and unsuitable, and the permanent housing may be even worse, as Beatrix Campbell found when she talked to young mothers in Wigan.[2] When councils finally manage to rehouse homeless people, they are often allocated to large and unattractive housing estates which are full of other single parents and families who have nowhere to go. Wendy and most of the other people from the hotel she was in were allocated flats on such an estate. Wendy's was on the ground floor of one of several high-rise blocks that stood bleak and isolated on the outskirts of a sprawling town. Kate and her two sons were allocated a flat on a vast estate full of other mothers and children in North London. She found it incredibly depressing to live there, but fortunately managed to get a place at college, a nursery for her two small children, and has since moved away to take a university course.

Kate was lucky in that she got out of her situation, but for many it is the beginning of a circle of deprivation and bad housing that is difficult to break, especially if you are on your own. Without the time or the qualifications to get a job with a decent wage, the only thing to do is to live on supplementary benefits. Another vicious circle is created for girls who have spent much of their lives already in 'care', in children's homes, those who have had severe family problems, or been convicted of some legal offence. A significant number get pregnant, go into a Mother and Baby Home, and may subsequently be given a flat in a deprived area. Some become pregnant again, their children may get taken into care, and the cycle continues.

Many girls cannot wait to get into a place of their own, they may be fed up with wherever they are living, whether it is their family home, a Mother and Baby Home, a bedsit or a hotel. Nickie's one dream was to get out of her bedsit and into her own flat. But even if this dream comes true, it can prove a great disappointment if you are all on your own. Life can get very hard and lonely, and you need more than the company of children, especially in the evenings. This is when the family may be a tower of strength and support. For those who have partners, life can be much better, unless of course you are so hard up you argue all the time, or he goes to the pub every night, or he hits you.

It has been suggested that some girls get pregnant specifically to get rehoused into a flat of their own. This may happen, although none of the mothers I talked to had done this. But with no propects of employment or housing, with nothing fulfilling on the horizon at all, getting pregnant is one meaningful direction to take. Few girls are likely to make such a calculated decision, but once they have got pregnant, if keeping the baby seems to offer the love and fulfilment that may be lacking in the rest of their lives, then being eligible for housing is obviously an added incentive. It is easy to criticise and condemn from a position of privilege. As an instance of rebellious motherhood rather than one of traditional maternity, it may get girls out of overcrowded family homes, and give them an accepted role with a baby who needs them.

Few young mothers live in their own house. Only those with a partner who has a stable and sufficient income, such as Lucy and Julie – both of whom had partners who were significantly older and in work – manage this. Claire and her young miner husband were renting a house while looking for one to buy. Jane was buying her own small house with a DHSS mortgage. The house had already been bought through her father-in-law before she and her husband split up. During the subsequent process of being evicted, she discovered that she could buy it herself.

Financially, the majority of teenage mothers find life a struggle. Although they, like any other mothers, are entitled to various benefits from the DHSS, these vary greatly according to age, where they are living, and with whom. These benefits tend to be inadequate and the logic of eligibility often seems inconsistent. Until recently, those under sixteen have been entitled only to the small maternity grant, child benefit and milk and vitamin tokens. With the new Social Security Act, under sixteen-year-olds lost this grant, and by April 1988 milk and vitamin tokens will be available only to those on supplementary benefit, which means those over sixteen.[3] The state acknowledges that babies have needs that cost money, but it does not recognise the needs of their mothers. Most mothers of this age have little option but to live with their parents, or be taken into care. Very occasionally they may live with their boyfriend. It is only at the magic age of sixteen that they become eligible for supplementary benefits and child benefit (including single-parent allowance if applicable). If they marry, any gain in Family Income Supplement that this brings is usually offset by the loss of single-parent allowance.[4] Those living with partners do not necessarily have an easier time, since if their boyfriend or husband is working he is quite likely to be young, relatively unskilled and on a low wage. If he is not working, they have to try and live off their joint social security payment. This calls for strict budgeting and does not allow for extras, or for things going wrong. Nor does it allow for irresponsible spending as when Doreen's husband took their money to drink in the pub, and Wendy's boyfriend spent their money on things for himself.

There is not much left over to spend on things like clothes, records, and going out. Wendy, living alone with her daughter, spends little on these, but tries to save for useful household things: 'I'm quite good really. I put £10 for my bills, £10 for clubs and stuff, £10 for shopping, and £4 for saving. My dad taught me to be good with money, I keep a little account book. I've just splashed out, and got some new jeans and some new shoes, but that's the first lot of new clothes I've had in ages.' Many girls depend on catalogues for buying things, or 'clubs', as do a lot of families without much ready money.

Lisa lives on the nineteenth floor of a block of flats in London with her eleven-month-old baby. The baby's father also lives there unofficially and, as he has a job, he gives her quite a lot of money to supplement her DHSS money. She shops, cooks, washes and irons his clothes like a traditional wife in return.

Nickie gave up her job when she got pregnant and, after having her baby prematurely, returned to her tiny bedsit for single girls, leaving her baby in the hospital. She has been told that it would take at least nine months to get her somewhere else to live. In debt and struggling to make ends meet on supplementary benefit, she sometimes wishes it had never happened:

> Going up to the hospital and seeing her, I'm glad I went through with it. Other times I'm bitter, and wish I hadn't. Why didn't I wait until I'm older, waited until I'm married, made sure I had money for the baby. Because now if she needs anything she'll have to wait. I can't go and buy it. If something happened, I don't even have the money to get a cab. I had a really good job and because of the baby they're not going to take me back. I wish I hadn't had her.

Living at home and getting a job while Mum looks after the baby is another solution, and one taken by Joanne and Bridget. Provided family relationships are harmonious, this is usually a comfortable and economical option for young mothers which provides some welcome financial independence. It is also economical for the DHSS, which would otherwise be paying out a lot more in rents and benefits. As it is, heating, electricity, food, clothes and other childcare costs are inevitably subsidised by the family.

BRIDGET

In Bridget's life, her lively two-and-a-half-year old son Steven comes first and her scooter comes second. They live with her parents and younger brother in a small council house on an estate on the outskirts of a Midlands town. She was only thirteen when she became pregnant, and her relationship with the baby's father was already splitting up. She started going out with a new boyfriend, who she soon told of her pregnancy, but she could not get round to telling her parents. In the end her boyfriend did it when she was about seven months. Her mother was upset and her father was angry, but they have given her help and support. At first her father would blame her for it every time they had an argument, but now he has mellowed and both parents treat Steven as if he were their own. Her father was working as a welder, but has given up work to look afer her mother, who recently had a heart attack. Her boyfriend stayed around for about a year until they moved house.

She went to school throughout her pregnancy, but was not allowed to go back after she had the baby, and she had a home tutor instead. For the last six months she has left Steven in the care of her mother while she took a job as a jigger and packer in a local factory, which has made her much happier than being on the dole. Although Bridget pays towards her keep, in terms of everything she receives from living at home, it is a bargain. It leaves her enough money left over to spend on things for her son and herself. Her main interest is scooters; the whole of one bedroom wall is papered with pages from scooter magazines, and having an income has meant that she could actually buy one. It also means she has money to pay her brother to babysit occasionally. Protected from the real costs of living, Bridget is reasonably well-off and happy and has no immediate plans for moving out.

'I hadn't a period for about three months, and I found I had liquid coming out of my breasts. I thought it was strange to start with, I didn't know what it was and then I started going through these books and reading about how you'd know that you were pregnant. So I eventually twigged that I was. I thought it would go away. I don't know why, I just thought if I forgot about it and went about life as normal. Then as I got later and later – it was difficult because I still had to go to school. I had to hide it really. I was petrified because a couple of months before my dad said if I ever did get pregnant he'd chuck me out. So I thought they would. That's why I left it so late I suppose.

My mum didn't say a lot when we told her, she burst out crying. She phoned my dad and she asked him to come home from work. Dad didn't really say a lot to me for a couple of days. He was cross. The doctor reckoned I was only about sixteen to twenty weeks pregnant. Then I had to go and have a scan, and the midwife came out and said I was thirty-three to thirty-four weeks pregnant. My mum just died of shock I think. Her mouth just opened. I wasn't really surprised. I knew the doctor was wrong when he said sixteen to twenty. But I didn't say anything at the time. It was a relief once everybody knew, I didn't have to hide it. My mum was helpful, she told me the right things to eat and took me down the doctor's. Got me some dresses. Horrible, but I had to wear them. At that time I liked wearing fashionable things, and they made me feel old. Big fly-away dresses. I didn't like going out.

My dad eventually asked me why I hadn't told anybody. Once we got over the first day of talking again, things seemed to be all right. I always had a better relationship with my dad than I did with my mum. I couldn't have a conversation with my mum without it turning into an argument. It was always like that. I used to sit down and talk to my dad most of the time. He did say that he was ashamed of me. But my dad keeps his feelings a lot to himself. I think my mum was upset that I didn't tell anyone. I don't think I get on as well now with my parents as we did before Steven was born. I'm supposed to be a mother now, so I think my dad expects me to dress and act like one. I dress comfortable, as my fashion is. I like having my hair short. But I don't think my dad agrees with that. He wants me to be like a mother should be. But I think whatever I look and dress like doesn't make any difference to how I react to Steven. But my mum doesn't moan at me the way my dad does about it. I like to go out of a night time. I go down and see my friends. When I go out I ask my brother to baby-sit for me usually. I can go out once Steven is asleep. I don't usually go till about half past eight. And come in about half past eleven.

I got depressed after I had him. But it did help having my boyfriend round. I think if I'd been totally on my own I think I would have lost contact with everything. He was quite happy to sit here of a night time with me and watch television, although he did sometimes go out. At first I was jealous because he used to go out on the scooter, and I wanted to do it but couldn't. But as time got on I knew it wouldn't change, so I just had to accept that I did have to stay in. It was tiring a lot of the time. Steven used to wake up at eleven o'clock at night and I used to be dead tired. I was dying to go to sleep and I had to sit there breastfeeding. I felt like getting a bottle of milk and giving it to him. And then again at four o'clock in the morning, and I really hated having to get up in the night with him. But after the first couple of months he slept longer through the night, and by three months he slept through. It's hard work. I didn't think it was going to be as bad as that.

I went on the pill after I stopped breastfeeding and I've been on it ever since. After I had Steven I wasn't interested in sex. I just went ever so funny. I couldn't be bothered. Kissing was all right but that was all. I think Dave, my boyfriend, understood how I felt. He never forced me into anything, he was really good about it. After I went on the pill something just clicked and I was interested in it again. I carried on seeing him for two years, after Steven was born, until we moved here. So we split up. Mum and Dad didn't like him anyway. But my dad's like that to all of them. Dad's a bit wary of all these weird haircuts. He called Dave a moron. He used to have his hair different colours different weeks. Blond one minute, black the next. They just didn't get on at all.

But Dave treated Steven like he was his own. He didn't mind taking him in the bath, and putting a clean nappy on him, but he hated changing dirty nappies. I didn't go out that often, but if I asked him to look after Steven he would. About a month after Steven was born he moved in with us because he got chucked out of his house. Mum and Dad were always pleasant to him, but I knew they didn't like him. But I didn't really care. There was me, Dave and Steven, and that's all I wanted at that time.

My brother and Dave used to sleep in one bedroom and I used to sleep in the other one. We weren't allowed to sleep together. I was only fourteen at the time. Even though I'd had the baby. But we did anyway. But I'm not so interested in boys really at the moment. I've got a lot of boyfriends, but only as friends. I'm a bit funny with boys at the moment. I'm much more cautious about going out with a boy now, after what happened. I go out about four or five times a week. I go to the disco Fridays. I do like going out doing things, because I get bored sitting in the house. My mum doesn't mind looking after Steven, but if I go out every night my dad starts moaning.

It's fantastic having a job. On social security I had about £20 a week and had to manage on it. Then I got this job, and get altogether about £75 a week – I couldn't believe how much money I was having. I didn't have to worry about borrowing money any more. If I want to buy Steven clothes or toys I can just go to the shop and get them. Before I couldn't. It's so much better. Mum looks after Steven during the day. I pay her £20 a week. So I have £55 left to myself and Steven. When I started that job it meant I could buy my scooter. It's all I ever wanted really, a scooter.

Mum does most of the work at home. I have to do the

housework on a Saturday. And I have to wash up the tea things of a night. Sometimes I do the ironing, but not very often. I hate it. I do the shopping more than I do the cooking. Dinner is usually ready for me when I come home. I used to do more before I got the job but I hated it. I get bored very quickly. I need something to occupy my mind. I get depressed if I've got nothing to do.

I wouldn't mind going to college and getting some qualifications but I'd rather go out and earn money. I'd rather give Steven things now than wait three years. He can't have everything because he hasn't got a dad. I think I have to make up for it. Steven knows me as his mum. Sometimes he'll call my mum, Mum. But he does know who his mum is. She's always made sure that I'm the one to look after him. More so when he was a little'un, really. But now he knows me as his mum it's easier to go out to work. He knows I come home at night. When I come through the door he gives me a kiss.

To start with I felt ashamed of being pregnant. But after he was born I thought, why should I care what anybody else thinks? He's mine, and if anyone wants to say anything that's up to them. I just get on with my life as it is. I thought, now I've got him I might as well enjoy him. People may say it's daft, but it's great to have a baby really. To know that he'll still be yours – I thought to myself when I'm nineteen he'll be starting school, and I won't really have started my life yet. While these other ladies are having their babies at nineteen or twenty, I'll be going out enjoying life more. And I've got something to show for it. I've got Steven. I was glad to have him in one sense, but not glad in other ways. I think mainly because of being so tied down at an early age. You have to grow up so much quicker. A lot of people said when they get older it gets harder. But I think it's the other way. It's much easier to live with Steven now than when he was a baby. Now I know that when he's asleep he'll stay asleep until I come home.

I'm comfortable here at the moment. I've got everything around me. I might stay here until he goes to school. I'm happy staying here. If I moved it's a problem of finding a childminder, and having to pay all your own bills, and your own food, and furniture. When I was younger I didn't want to tell people he was mine, but I like to now. I'm proud of him, and I know Mum and Dad are too. I don't care what happens as long as Steven's all right. I like seeing him happy. I like it when I come in and he gives me a kiss. He definitely comes first, and my scooter second.

KATE

Kate's council flat is one of many scattered in square clumps over a vast and desolate housing estate in London. She lived there with her two young sons, Philip, aged four and Luke, aged three; one of many single parents who are allocated homes on this estate. She had just finished doing her A-levels at college when she talked to me, which she passed and has since left London to take a university course and make a new life for herself and her children.

She met Neil, her sons' father, when she was fifteen and he was nineteen. He was her first boyfriend and she thought him very exciting and worldly. They spent a lot of time getting drunk and having a good time, she wasn't interested in school then. Her parents had divorced when she was about seven years old, and she remembers her and her brothers growing very independent as her mother studied for her O- and A-levels and then a degree. She was not very close to either of her parents then, but she and her mother have become closer since Kate went back to college.

Throwing away the contraceptive pills her mother gave her, she drifted into and through pregnancy, living with her boyfriend's family. Her eldest son was only a few months old when she became pregnant again, at the age of seventeen. When her second son was about a year old she moved to this flat, which was miserable, isolating and very cold in the winter. Her boyfriend, who was unemployed, also lived there at first, but his boredom and apathy was very depressing and Kate could feel herself going the same way. So when she started college she asked him to leave. He went back to his mother's where he sadly degenerated, and some time later committed suicide.

' My mother was so liberal with me, she allowed my boyfriend to stay, she was very easygoing. It must have been awful for her because I had thrown all her niceness back in her face and got pregnant. I think she was quite upset about that, and because I was so young. She was very nice about it, although she said she didn't want me to stay at home, because she was teaching. I didn't like her very much at the time, and I didn't want to stay, so I moved in with my boyfriend. His parents were absolutely delighted about it. They'd bought the pram even before the tests were through.

I didn't think about getting pregnant a great deal, I don't know why I thought I wouldn't, we never used any contraception. It was just doing our thing, racing about and getting drunk all the time. It was just part of everything else we did. It was all very thoughtless and rash, but I was enjoying myself. I didn't want school. I didn't want to work. My mother gave me a supply of pills which I never took. She just presented them to me – these will stop you getting pregnant. There were just a few packets, and I think she thought if I took them regularly I'd continue with them myself, go and get more myself. I flushed them down the loo. I must have got pregnant just about then. I must have been determined to reject everything that she wanted. I think me and my brothers all learned to do our

135

own things because she was at work or doing her degree. We didn't really see much of her. She'd be going out as we came in. We all did our own washing, things like that. I always felt domesticated from an early age. We were all very independent really.

I drifted through pregnancy, I just didn't think about it at all. I had the baby and he was very nice and very small and didn't moan and cry. He slept through the night and it was very pleasant having him and it meant I didn't have to go to work which was nice. I'd just left school. I wasn't really there much towards the end anyway. I decided I didn't really want to do O-levels, I didn't want to do anything. It was a nice excuse at the time.

Neil was as blasé as I was about it all, he was quite pleased actually, something to do with his manhood, his virility. And he was very good. He used to play with Philip for hours, and feed him and change his nappies. If he wasn't doing that he was out drinking. He didn't talk to me much, but I must admit he was very nice to Philip. We didn't live together very long, and when I was at his mum's he didn't do anything for me. He was a nice bloke, he just wasn't very thoughtful. He used to buy me sweets, but that was all. He never did any domestic work.

He typified the skinhead, anti-everything, yet he was very gentle, he wasn't violent at all. I think he was really into settling down while still retaining his old habits of going out drinking. He wanted to be a father but he didn't want to commit himself all the way. He used to spend the dole money as well, so in the end I had to tell the Social Security that he'd run off so I could have my own money. He never had a permanent job. I don't know what he did half the time. He always managed to get a job if he had a reason, like going to court, but not for long. He went to court for various things, right from when I first met him – speeding, taking and driving away, then I think he got caught for forgery, petty things.

Then I got pregnant again, two months after I had Philip.
I felt so embarrassed. How could anyone be so stupid. I
didn't mind because I liked the idea, but I was thinking of
everyone else. Philip could barely walk and I was almost
having Luke. Walking down the street you could see
people trying to work it out. Teenage spots and two
children. When I had Philip I felt really motherly and
happy and my face was glowing. But with Luke, Philip was
jumping about and Luke was terribly heavy to carry, and
I just felt so silly. You could see people saying, how could
she make the same mistake twice.

I felt more terrified with Luke than with Philip. I think
I was justifying it by saying, yes it's good to have children
while you're still young. But I was very scared, and I was
being pushed into getting married. I was almost married
but I had to assert myself. Neil didn't really want to get
married, it was his mother who wanted this.

After I had Luke I was quite pleased that I had two
children, but then I moved up here, where I didn't know
anyone and I got terribly bored. I spoke to my social
worker, one of many, and she found a day nursery for the
boys. Luke was about a year old then and Philip two, so
they went to nursery and I went to college. I'd always felt
kind of led, sort of put into a category, and it fulfilled it
when I moved here. It's one of those places that people talk
about. No one gets sent here unless you're a single parent.
People assume what you're like – you can't look after your
children, they'll roam the streets, that sort of thing. People
are always surprised when they see how content the boys
are. They're so suspicious, they look at the children for
signs. I was always in fear of my children being taken away.
I was always desperately careful they didn't bump their
heads or whatever. I thought a bruise was enough for them
to be dragged off. But they're happy. I don't let them go out

on their own, so they don't see much of this place, and they're at nursery all day.

Luke wasn't quite a year old when I moved up here and it was so boring. I was here on my own. Everything got to be such a drag. I used to lie here all day and watch them play on the floor, and they were bored with me. It was horrid, I felt like a middle-aged woman with two kids. I just felt very bored by it all. I looked awful and felt awful. I felt old and very lonely. I thought I'd never socialise again. Neil had gone by then. Then I went to college and I was mixing with people of about eighteen and everyone was full of admiration for me and I couldn't see why. It opened up a whole new social life for me, including the boys, I used to take them to college sometimes. It was a novelty for them at college, someone with two kids.

It became nicer to spend the evening with the boys instead of the whole day. It's the quality I think, and now it's me that prolongs it, they fall asleep on me! It's so desolate up here. If I had to stay here all day I think I'd go mad. It's so vast and impersonal. You can't get out of here unless you have another baby or your house blows up. It's more likely to be your house blowing up, some of the things are so old and dangerous. The winter's awful, I just wanted to cry all the time. It's freezing cold and I'm frightened of the heating in case it blows up or bankrupts me. We all go to bed with our clothes on. I take my work to bed with me. The mornings when you go out it's dark and you come back in the dark, it's depressing. That's why I took A-levels, I wanted to do something.

After I had Luke I went on the pill. I'd definitely grown up by then. It would have been disastrous to have another child – I'd really planned to go back to college after Philip, but I seem to make the best of my mistakes. I knew it was time to pull myself together. Sometimes I wish I'd taken the Pill when my mum gave it to me, when the boys

138

have been naughty or something. But on the whole I'm pleased I've done it this way. If I get into university it will all have been worth it. When I'm thirty they'll be teen-agers. It won't be so bad.

My mum and I have a very nice relationship now that I've done A-levels and she teaches. We can talk about the books and things. During the exams I used to phone her, and she's nice to the boys as well. At the time I was desperate to get out, but sometimes I wish I could just be one of the family. But I quite like it on my own. It's made me more independent. I couldn't even think about going and living with anyone.

The boys are so good, they never grumble, sometimes I think they're older than they are. I read them stories before bed, which takes a good hour, then I give them a stack of books in bed while I get on with my work. I didn't pamper them at all. I used to play with them a lot. It definitely doesn't fulfil your whole life to have a child, not for me anyway. I love them now, I don't really think I loved them before, I was too bored by it all, I think, and too depressed. Now I spend less time with them, I really enjoy them, they're very nice. I think I love them so much because they talk to me. I love their idiosyncracies, it's not just because they're mine.

I think I've made the best of what I've done. I'm really happy now. I'm a lot stronger than I was, more independent, and I'm more demanding now. If I don't know something I go and find out about it rather than let it pass, things like Social Security. I'm not so passive. You have to push for things, especially with young children because people label you with all the usual things that come with being a single parent.

JANE

Jane lives in her own little house on a neat housing estate in the south-east of England with her two-year-old son Ben, and a lodger. She works as a waitress occasionally to make ends meet, and is very involved with a local group set up specifically for young mothers like herself.

She was doing a nursery nursing course at college when she got pregnant. Waiting until she was sixteen to go to the clinic for the Pill because she thought she wouldn't be allowed to have any before, she was already a week late with her period by the time her appointment came through. The baby's father, in his mid-twenties, offered to look after her but she didn't want this, although she knew she wanted the baby.

She went to live with her mother at first, who had reacted calmly and stood by her. Her parents had divorced when she was about seven. She was looked after by a nanny when she was little, but because she kept skipping off school, she was sent to boarding school. There she got six O-levels and could have stayed on longer, but decided to take the nursery nursing course instead.

When she was four months pregnant she met her husband, Chris, who moved in with her after two weeks and they got married after the baby was born. Her husband's father put up the money for them to get a house, where they lived for a while until Chris started going out with other women and she eventually told him to leave. He did, but then the question arose of how she and her son could carry on living in the house.

'If my solicitor hadn't suggested it, I'd never have thought of buying the house. You don't, when you're on the dole. You don't think you can get a mortgage. You do have to have someone that can guarantee your mortgage.

Someone who owns a business, that can be good enough.
I don't know what I would have done if I hadn't been living
here. If I'd been evicted, I'd never have bought a house.
It's been hard work, and it's a worry too. The 'Social' pay
the interest, but they don't pay it direct, they give you the
money and you have to pay it. When I get that cheque, I
want to spend it so much. But I have to be responsible.

When I got together with my husband, before we were
married, we were to move into a bed and breakfast because
no landlord would take us. It was all we could get. It was a
disgusting place, really horrible. It was two little rooms
and it was £45 a week, plus £10 to have my baby there. The
council would have paid the rent. For that they could buy
a massive place. They wouldn't find us a council place but
they would have paid that. We weren't on the list,
we weren't eligible. We were living at my mum's, but we
didn't want to stay there. It's very difficult when you're
living with somebody else. We only had one room, it was
like a basement flat. The room was damp. It was all right in
the summer, but by the start of the winter it was damp.
Chris's dad, he's really rich, and said he'd buy us a house to
live in. It would be in his dad's name but we'd live in it.

We found this place and bought it, but when I split up
with my husband, his dad wanted me to move out. But you
just can't find a house. You can't get council
accommodation. There's a two-year waiting list with the
housing association. So I said, "You'll have to evict me
then", so he started to do that. I really didn't expect it.
I thought he wouldn't do it. That's when my solicitor said,
'Why don't you buy it?' I went to a building society.
Luckily one had just merged with another building society
and they had money available. They even had a notice up
– "We have money at the moment for mortgages." I got a
mortgage, just like that! Obviously there was a form to
sign, and it was hilarious, it just didn't apply to me. How

much do you earn, that sort of thing. So I put a letter in with it saying that I knew I could pay it.

I don't know anything about houses, except they are an investment. The DHSS pays the interest. But it's a problem, because if I worked too much then I lose my benefit. And if I had a job at about £100 a week, I couldn't pay the mortage and live. Although it's £33,000, my mortgage is for £30,000, and I've had to put a down payment on it. I just borrowed and begged. My relatives, they haven't got much money but they've all got a bit. My grandma came up with an insurance policy.

At the time I was pregnant, my mum was buying a house, so I thought I might as well move in there. I knew I was pregnant in the October, but I didn't tell her until January. I didn't want to spoil Christmas. I briefly thought about abortion but I thought, no. I thought, I don't need to, I'll be all right. I thought whatever happens I'll be all right. And a baby turned up! My mum was wonderful. I went in and sat there with a long face, hoping she'd say, 'What's the matter?' But she said, 'Are you pregnant?' I said, 'Well, yes I am.' She said, 'Well, there's nothing I can do now. A baby isn't a bad thing. The bad thing is that you're having a baby now at sixteen while you're at college. It's a stupid thing to do. I could say I'll throw you out, but I'm going to have a grandchild, and I can't do that. It's not the child's fault. So if you actually have it I might as well stand by you.' She was so marvellous. It's the nicest she could have been.

College was the biggest thing in my life and that's what she was most upset about. They said I could have a year off. But if I'm going to have a baby I think I might as well look after it. Some kids, if they have a baby at sixteen and they haven't worked, it can be quite frightening when they do get out of the house to do something to try and be independent. It's hard work working when you've got kids anyway. I think part of me thought, Oh, I don't have to go out to work, I can stay at home and look after the baby. I should have known what it was like to look after kids, the kind of work I did. But you always think you can do it better than anyone else. I don't regret having him, but if I could turn the clock back, or if someone came to me and said, 'Is it a good idea to have a baby at sixteen?' I'd say no. It's a question of knowing a bit more about yourself. Suddenly you're second place. You're your parents' daughter, and suddenly you're a mother. You haven't had that time in between just for you. Even now I don't know what I'm doing really. Sometimes I think, oh, this is my child. It's still not real. Sometimes I think I'm playing a game. It's as if someone will come along and say, "Oh, I'll look after him now." To take the responsibility for a bit. I do get babysitters, but you've still got it in your head.

I never know why I got married really. It was crazy. At the time, the reasons were ridiculous. The tax, things like that. It might have worked, but he was a real sod. It's one thing I look back on and I don't even know why I did it. Because it was the grown-up thing to do I suppose. And I didn't want to be the young single mother. I didn't want, like at the Health Centre, for them to call out "Miss". However free-thinking I was, I didn't like it. I was seventeen when we got married, in a registry office. It was a horrible wedding. It's so quick. You don't feel married after something like that. You have to really know someone before sharing your life with them. Whatever happened, we said we'd get through it, and I was quite prepared to do that. Chris was too. But he did see other women, and I didn't want it anymore. So I threw him out. It was like having two babies, and I was only a baby myself. So I decided I'd be better off on my own.

People look at me and say, "She's wasted her life", but there's little things I've done. Like the women's group I help with. I'm so proud of that. There's not a lot I can do. I can't go out and get a fantastic job, so I get involved in little things like that, and they've given me so much. It started from nothing. It took £25 to start the group from Social Services, and now we've got our own flat, a childminder to look after the kids, and paid workers to run the group. When I was with Chris I was working, but it was difficult when we split up and I had to find a childminder. It was only waitressing but it's a nice place. But then my childminder said she was going strawberry-picking, so I haven't worked for three weeks. But now I've got my lodger and she's going to babysit. I shall work nights and Ben will hardly know I've gone. It's better at night. But it's hard when you have to rely on someone else. But I need to go out to some kind of job, otherwise you become a mother and nothing else.

One thing I like about working, you walk around without the buggy. But I'll go and buy nappies and things. I have to let people know, because it's the only thing I've done that's maybe a bit different from everyone else. It's silly, because nobody really cares. I just hope I don't have any more babies, but if I know me, I will. I don't regret having Ben. He's special, he's mine. I've been so lucky. I always land on my feet. I don't know why. I have had family support, not so much with Ben, but with getting a home. There aren't many girls who get pregnant at sixteen, and in two years have a nice house and a mortgage.

7
MARRIAGE

Men and women get married, unmarried and remarried with great frequency. For pregnant teenagers, marriage may be an option if they are over sixteen, but 'shot-gun weddings', when couples are forced to marry, are by and large a thing of the past. Although marriage is still seen as the most appropriate place to have sex and children, I have the impression that more parents are now likely to advise a young pregnant daughter to wait until she is sure she wants to marry, even if she is definite about having and keeping her baby. In the ten years between 1970 and 1980, the number of pregnant teenagers who got married was halved.[1] Nevertheless, a substantial number of young girls do marry when they get pregnant, or soon after having the baby, especially in the 18–19-year-old age group.[2]

Research into the backgrounds of teenage parents show a tendency for many of them to come from families in which parents have separated or divorced. Their own futures, according to the figures, are not much rosier. Teenage brides are twice as likely to end up being divorced as those aged 20 to 24-years-old, and four times as likely as those aged 25 to 29-years-old.[3] Three of the mothers in this book were already divorced before leaving their teens. The conditions under which many such marriages start out contribute to this. The social and economic limitations of low wages and unemployment and inadequate housing take their toll on love's young dream. The novelty of having an independent life together wears thin. Loving care and concern turn to resentment with the relentless demands of everyday life. Depression is a common characteristic of young mothers with children at home.[4]

It is considered that girls generally mature earlier than boys in all sorts of ways, and many young mothers discover that their teenage boyfriends or husbands are unable to handle this situation. Whether you are married or living together, it is not easy to take on the responsibility for other people's lives, especially if you are still working out your own. It is during this period, often classified under the broad label of adolescence, that many people are struggling to discover their own self identity, and are going through a number of quite confusing physical and psychological changes. To combine this with being a parent trying to financially and emotionally maintain a family can prove very hard work, and can certainly break up a marriage or any similar relationship.

Maybe it is significant then, that two mothers who expressed great contentment and happiness were well-housed and provided for by their partners, who in each case were in their thirties and employed. Neither of them were currently married to their partners, but both intended to be. Julie was eighteen with a nine-month-old daughter. She had met her fiancé two years before. They'd just bought a little terraced house in Yorkshire. The age difference between them is larger than that between Julie and her baby. Lucy, with a six-month-old daughter, had been living in the country with her boyfriend for a year, since her sixteenth birthday. She'd known him since she was nine, and 'I always thought he was lovely. I prayed every night that he wouldn't get married.' They'd got close when her parents split up a few years before, and their relationship had developed from there.

Marie's marriage landed her in a Home for Battered Wives. No matter how much I hear about domestic violence, I still feel surprised at how often this had been a feature within these teenage mothers' own relationships or those of their parents. It isn't just something that happens in 'other' families, it can happen almost anywhere, especially if conditions are frustrating and tough. All too often men take it out on women. Wendy's boyfriend sometimes hit her when they lived together, and she put up with it for a long time. Marie had thought she could help her husband to come out of it, but she was wrong.

Only a few of the mothers contributing to this book are, or have been married; among the few that had been, each had married while she was pregnant or soon after the baby was born. Jane's son was several months old when she married her boyfriend, who was not the baby's father. Doreen felt pressured into it by her parents, Marie was in a romantic dream, and for both it turned out to be a mistake. Claire is still happily married. She had known her husband for over a year when she got pregnant and they had already talked about getting married one day.

A few were living with their boyfriends on a permanent basis, either on their own or in their parents' home. The line between marriage and living together can be quite a narrow one. The conditions and experiences of daily life can be exactly the same even if the legal commitments are different. The general attitudes towards marriage were positive. No matter how aware girls are of the grim realities of other peoples' marriages, they believe it can be different for them.[5] Although many of them came from single-parent families, and they themselves had been through a disappointing relationship, only a minority were totally against it. The rest were either in favour of it, or they felt it was all right, and perhaps they would marry later if the right person came along. But most were clear that they would not get married just because they were pregnant.

CLAIRE

Despite the pessimistic figures, not all teenage marriages break up, and everyone optimistically believes that things will work out differently for them. In Claire's case, this may be true. She was seventeen when she was married, and five months pregnant. She had previously been doing a hairdressing job and was on day release as part of a youth training scheme.

She started going out with Mark, her husband, when she was fourteen, he was her first proper boyfriend. Having risked getting pregnant for about a year, her mother suggested she went on the Pill. But she had a lot of trouble finding one that suited her, and it was on changing pills that she got pregnant.

With her son Bobby now twenty months old, she is pregnant again, something both she and her twenty-year-old husband want. They live in a mining area of the Midlands where they rent a little three-bedroomed house, paid for with his wages from working down the pit, and so far things seem to be working out quite well.

'Mum didn't like Mark very much when she first saw him, because he was a skinhead. In fact, the first time she saw him he had no shirt on, he'd got 'Doc Martens' boots up to about there, got no hair, but once she knew him she liked him.

I'd always wanted kids. The woman I worked for used to think I was stupid as all I used to talk about was babies and houses. I was going out with Mark then. Me and Mark had talked about the possibility that I might get pregnant but it was years ahead, we thought. We weren't really bothered. He'd have stuck by me, he wouldn't have let me have an abortion because he doesn't hold with them. He's always loved kids. I was fifteen when we first did it and I'd known

Mark five months. I didn't like it. It hurt and I couldn't see what all the excitement was about. Then it changed. I think it's when you start loving each other more and get used to each other. I think your expectations are more. You read about people and it's all loving – it never happens like you expect it to. Everybody I've talked to, they've all said it was a let-down.

I was ten weeks when I found out I was pregnant. I kept thinking I was. We'd been on holiday with my mum and dad and when we got there I had some tea and I felt sick, and my mum just looked at me. When I got back, I started putting weight on, and she says, "You're not pregnant, are you?" "Oh no, definitely not." But one night I just told her, and went to doctors next day, and he said yes, you definitely are. I felt quite happy about it but I was only sixteen so I was a bit frightened, but it was what I wanted. His mum went absolute crazy – I'd got to have an abortion, she was having nowt to do with it, and if we didn't get married she'd have nowt to do with us, she went through everything, she was horrible really. She's totally different now with Bobby, now she worships him. As soon as we got married she started being all right.

My mum told my dad, and he just said what happened to the Pill? I expected him to go really crazy but he just says, "Well, when are you getting married?" because they all wanted us to get married, and we wanted to as well.

When I got married I was about five months pregnant but it didn't show. There's only one photo when you can tell. We're stood in the doorway of the church and it's sort of silhouetted and you can see through my dress there's this little lump, but it could be the hoops on the underskirt, it's just that I think its that, but that's the only one you can tell anything. There was no problem having a white wedding, the vicar knew. That's what I wanted. My dad said if I could either have a wedding, or money, but I wanted to get married and have a nice wedding. I think Mark would've got married in a Registry Office, he wasn't very bothered, but that's what I wanted and that's what I got. It was lovely. I cried all the way down the aisle, I couldn't talk. Mark was dead calm and I was just a nervous wreck. There were about a hundred came in the day and about two hundred at night, there were a lot there.

When we got married we lived at my mum's. It was all right but I think we were glad to get out and I think they were glad for us to go, but we got on all right; I think we just made ourselves get on. Bobby was about eight weeks old when we moved out, because Mum wanted us to stop until I had him and I was sorted out.

I had a good pregnancy really. I was just enormous, and with being so small it looked even bigger. I went very big as soon as we married. I just lumped it on, it was as though it waited for me to get married and then it just expanded. Having him was really easy, there were no problems at all. I went to the hospital at half past six and I had him at twenty to nine. I was really lucky having him. He was lovely when he was born. You can't believe that that baby is actually yours, nobody could take it off you. It was like having someone of your own, someone who would love you back.

Being married has it's ups and downs. I get fed up sometimes, when I can't go out, and all my friends are coming round. Although I do get out, I work in a pub two nights a week so that gets me out. I worked mornings too, but when I found out about the new baby I cut down as it's a really busy pub, and it was tiring me out too much. On a Saturday night Bobby goes down to Mark's mum and stops the night and then we go down on Sunday. I work Fridays and Sundays, so Mark stops in with him then. On Saturday Mark will go out with his friends and I'll go out with my friends. We don't go out together very often, we see enough of each other during the day!

Mark's ever so good. He'll do anything for Bobby, he'll do anything I ask him really, sometimes he moans but he'll do it in the end. When I was having Bobby he'd read all the books. He knew more about having him than I did! He's always changed his nappies for him and bathed him.

He's always been one of the lads, that's really why we don't go out together. He's got all his mates, goes to football matches, things like that. I don't think he would have got married so soon, but I don't think he'd part with Bobby now.

My dad always said I could have £1000 when I was twenty-one, but since I got married before this, he said I could have it then, so we bought most of the furniture and everything out of that, and out of the money we'd saved, and wedding presents, we had loads of wedding presents. We had a washer on HP but that's the only thing. We had telly off his mum and dad, and we had a cleaner off my grandma and grandad. We just manage really on what we've got now.

At the pub I get about £20 for three sessions. We could manage without it, but it gets me out of the house a bit. That makes me feel better. It makes you feel you've got to be bothered as well, I mean you've got to look decent to go and things like that so you make an effort more. I think you go through stages when you can't be bothered with yourself, you're that busy with the house and you're not bothered about anything, only looking after the baby.

I spend my days shopping and cleaning up. If I've got nowt to do there's a big pond down there and there's all ducks on it and a field full of horses and cows so I take Bobby down there, but usually by the time I've done all housework and sorted him out, Mark's home. I go up to my mum some afternoons. Mark's home at half past one when he's on days but he wants to go to bed then, he's tired, so I'm just sat down here playing with Bobby. In the evening we watch telly, there's usually somebody comes down, one of his mates or one of mine. You can't really go far cos I like Bobby to go to bed early, so that's all you can do.

Looking back, sometimes I wish it hadn't happened because I feel like I've not had much of a life. When I'm at work and I see everybody going out, girls with the lads and that and I think I've never had none of that, I've always been with Mark. But we've got a nice house, and I don't think if I had to go over it again I'd change what's happened. I think I'd have made it a bit later though. I was a bit young. I think I would have liked to have got my City and Guilds in hairdressing before having my baby.

I think if somebody wanted to get pregnant, they want to think very seriously about it because it's a lot different to what you expect. You don't have this baby that just lies there and looks lovely – it changes your life totally. You've got no time to yourself. When you're not married and you've got no kids you can just go and sit in your bedroom and paint your toenails and make yourself all nice, but with a kid you don't get time to do nothing, you don't even get a bath. You don't get a chance to just sit down and read or do anything else, they're always there. But I'm very lucky to have a husband, family and friends who care about me and love me. I've got a wonderful son and my life is just perfect.

DOREEN

Doreen was not so lucky with her marriage. At nineteen, she is now divorced, and lives with her three children – two sons aged four and three and a ten-month-old daughter – in a council house in the West of England. She got pregnant at fifteen and married her eighteen-year-old boyfriend Terry six months after her son was born. She was not at all bothered about being pregnant. She had never felt very loved by her parents, and felt that she was

152

always compared unfavourably to her sister. She knew she wanted the baby.

She was still at school at first, but did not enjoy it very much as the other kids kept talking about her behind her back. At about five months pregnant she left school and had a home tutor, which she enjoyed much more. Before they were married she and Terry lived in her parents' house, which was rather overcrowded. It was her parents who put pressure on her and her boyfriend to get married.

Believing it was a good idea to have a second child quite soon, she got pregnant again and it was soon after this that the marriage went wrong. Terry lost his job, he went out every night and drank their money away. Her third pregnancy was an accident, and she became terribly depressed about it. It was at this point that she determined to get divorced and make a life of her own.

'If, when you're about fourteen or so, you let the boys all have sex with you, they call you a slag, and if you don't, they say you're tight and not worth going out with. That's why I never had many boyfriends. I wouldn't let them have sex. Then Terry came along, and I did with him. I'd been going with him about a year. When he wanted sex first, I said no. He kept on, so I said only if he used the sheath. I didn't know anything about the Pill, how to go about getting it, and I couldn't talk to my mum about it. So he used the sheath. Then, I didn't realise he'd stopped using it at first. And I didn't seem to worry about it for some reason. I was always arguing with my parents, they nagged me all the time. They let my sister off. It was always me. I suppose I thought if I had a baby, I'd get out of all that. Then when I found I was pregnant, I wasn't really bothered about it. I was worried about what my parents would do, but I wasn't upset. I wanted the baby. Mum had never explained anything. I got everything from books. When I got

153

pregnant, I thought I was and I went in the school library
and looked up everything I could about finding out if you
were pregnant. I thought I'd got all the symptoms, so I
must be pregnant. I didn't tell my parents. The doctor did.
I was too scared. It was Christmas, and Mum didn't want to
tell my dad over Christmas. So she told him New Year's
Day. And he was over the moon about it! That made my
mum pleased. So then it was all plans, and baby clothes
and things. I was only fifteen and they weren't worried at
all. But they did take over a bit, which I didn't like. After
the baby was born, when I arrived home my mum rushed
out, grabbed the baby, and ran indoors with him. It went
on like that for two months or so until it ended in a blazing
row. I told them, it's my baby and I'm going to look after it.
After that, they got the message.

There were five of us children living at home then. Me
and Tina were in together with the baby. We didn't have
much room. My two elder brothers had a bedroom, and my
younger brother had a room of his own, but that was a tiny
little room. I was glad when I moved out because it was
getting too much to handle. My sister moaned because the
baby cried at night. Mum moaned because I put the light
on at night, because I breastfed him. Have you ever tried
breastfeeding a baby in the pitch black? Terry lived there
but we couldn't have the same bedroom, there wasn't the
room. So it was like having a boyfriend. More like a brother
I suppose really. He used to see the baby and play with
him, but it wasn't like living together. Not like a proper
husband or father. He's never really taken on the role of
father, never played with them. I think he thought of
babies as things that were stuck in a pram and fed.

When my parents started getting a bit heavy, they said
would Terry like to get engaged, and he said yes. So he
bought a ring and that. Then we found out we'd got a
house. We'd had our names down just to live together. But

then my parents started nagging. What will people say, that sort of thing. So I said shall we get married, and he said yes. I think it was mainly because of the pressure we were under to get married. His parents couldn't really care less, because they didn't really like me. They thought I'd trapped him but I gave him the choice. When I knew I was pregnant I said you can get out now, or are you going to stay? And he decided to stay. So it was his own decision. I would have been happy to have the baby, on my own. Terry was a friend of my brothers'. That's how we met. He was always there with them. But I honestly don't know how we managed to do it without getting caught. My mum was working nights till nine or ten, Dad was out working. I suppose that's how we did it. But there was always such a lot of people in the house.

I sometimes felt that my parents didn't love me enough. They used to pick on me, saying I should grow up. But then as soon as you are grown up, they want you to be a kid again. You can't win. They didn't have time for me. Mum wouldn't communicate with me, and I felt really pushed out and neglected. I felt unwanted. And then I met Terry and I suppose I clung to him because he gave me the affection that I needed. I did love Terry, really, a lot. Then the way he treated me after we married, made it turn into hate. I can't stand him now. He used to threaten me, and every night he'd be out spending our money. We never used to see him, and when we did, he used to pick arguments. It was hell. Now, I feel really bitter towards him. I gave up everything to be his wife, and have his children, and then he turned round and did all that. I felt cheated out of my teenage life. I could have been out myself instead of being a good little housewife. I get out more now. I've been out more in the past six months than I did for the three years I was with him.

Terry always drank a lot, down the pub. I think it's

because he used to see all his old mates there, from school, and he wanted to do what they did. In a way he wanted us but he still wanted his old bachelor life. Do all the things his mates were doing, and after a while he forgot about us. I didn't think that was right. I gave up everything, I just wanted a happy family life. He wanted to still have a good time but to come home to a wife and family and his tea on the table. I told him to choose, and he chose that. So out he went. So then I had to pull myself together and get on with the job, which I did. I'm glad I did too. I didn't want the kids to end up in a home, I wanted them to have a mother at least, if they couldn't have a father.

I got pregnant with Sarah through missing one day's Pill. It shows how easy it can be. I was depressed after that, because I didn't want any more children. I'd had a part-time job for about six weeks when I found out. When I'm first pregnant I get ill, fainting and that, so I couldn't carry on working. It was only in a factory, packing pet products. But it was work. So I gave up my job. My marriage was really terrible then. Terry lost his job, and that made it worse. He used to do painting and decorating for a building firm, then he lost his job just before Christmas. Christmas was terrible. I was on tablets from the doctor, I couldn't talk to anybody. That was the worst thing. Not being able to talk to anybody. My mum wanted my marriage to work out, and I felt as though I had to prove to her that it could work. I had to live up to their image they wanted of me. There's never been a divorce in my family before. I'm the black sheep of the family now. Mum keeps going on to me – 'It's a pity you ever got married in the first place' – but it's because of them that I got married, because they didn't want us to live together, they didn't want me to live on my own because they felt I was too young, so I got married just to please them really, which was wrong. But I was so fed up with people telling me what to do. I just had to get out of the situation. So I got married, to run away from it, I think. And got myself into a worse mess than before.

But once I'd made the decision to kick him out, get divorced, I was really happy. I felt as though a weight had come off my shoulders. Mum didn't want me to do it, saying it would work out. I said it wouldn't, and told her everything that had happened. I kicked Terry out, and everybody thought we'd get back together again. But I said no way am I going back. I'm not doing anything for anybody else. I'll do it my way now. The hardest part is going out again, getting used to seeing people. My sister dragged me down the pub and that. I felt really out of place at first. But now I know them all, it's great.

Some people think that because you're young and have a baby you should give up everything. That you should be adult straight away. Well you are, you're torn between being a teenager and being a responsible person. When you're at home you have to be responsible, with the kids, but when you're out you have to join in with people of your own age. It's weird. I'm used to it now. When I'm at home I'm quite adult, although I still have a laugh. But when I'm out I make sure I have a good time. I don't just sit there in the background. I want to be with people my age. I've got to let off steam sometimes. But I've also got to be adult for the kids. Most of the people I go out with are younger, they're not married, they haven't got kids. So they don't want to know about my life. So I just talk about pop music and things like that. Next day they're probably the same, but I have to be adult and responsible again. It was difficult at first, but I'm used to that now. I think I've grown up a lot. I've had to. Having babies makes you grow up, but going through a bad marriage and a divorce makes you grow up too. I've come to terms with the situation now.

Terry has to give me maintenance, and he's got to pay off all the debts he ran up. I'm on Social and Family

Allowance. It works out at £62 a week to run the house and feed us. I manage. I budget everything out every week. I don't really get time for things like shopping for clothes. At night I relax. I have a bath, watch TV, read the paper. I usually read today's paper tomorrow, I'm usually behind. It would be different if there was a husband to help. You have to do everything yourself.

I'd advise any other girl to make your own decisions. When you get pregnant at that age everybody tells you what to do. Your parents, your boyfriend, all push you into doing things, and you're so muddled. I think you've got to go away on your own for a couple of hours and think it through, and when you've got it straight in your own mind, go and tell them then. And stick to it, that's the main thing. I think that's important. I only got married to get out of a situation, and it wasn't right. If people had left me alone, I'd have been all right all along. I'd say, if you've got a really good boyfriend and he sticks by you and you make the right decision, you'll be all right and you'll have been lucky. I don't think you should stick it out if you're unhappy. If I'd still been with Terry now, I would have been really miserable, and the kids would have been miserable, but because I made the decision to get divorced, everybody's happy. And I like living on my own. You can do what you want, the house is yours, you don't have to answer to anybody else. You don't have to ask if you can spend money on this or that. I don't regret getting married, because if I hadn't I wouldn't have Katie or Sarah. We did have good times, as well as bad. I think Terry loved me in his own way, although he still wanted his own life. But things are working out well now.

MARIE

Marie is twenty and her son Jamie is three. They live on the east coast of England, in a two-bedroomed maisonette on a private estate, obtained through the council. She became pregnant at sixteen, when she was changing over pills, and married her eighteen-year-old boyfriend Steve when she was four months pregnant. She had left school at fifteen after passing five CSEs and got a job in a supermarket.

Her mother is white and her father comes from Jamaica. They did not get married until Marie was three years old. Nevertheless, although her mother was helpful when she was pregnant, her father would not have anything to do with her. This hurt her as they had always been close before. Her parents are both strict Jehovah's Witnessess, as Marie was until she was about fourteen.

Abandoning plans for the army, Steve became unemployed, and being stuck in a flat all day together, the marriage soon started deteriorating. When he began to hit her she did not tell anyone, but went to her family doctor to try and help him. When he started hitting their son she left and went to a battered wives home, and started divorce proceedings.

She gets very depressed and feels extremely bitter over everything that has happened. She feels bored and totally trapped. After she had her son he went into special care for a while and she felt as if she had not had a baby. She remained detached, had postnatal depression, and still does not feel strong affectionate bonds with him. The year before she had arranged to have him fostered, but could not go through with it in the end.

The only permissible reason for divorce in her parents' religion is adultery, and therefore Marie's divorce was not recognised in their eyes. When she started seeing other men this was seen as fornication, and she was dis-fellowshipped.

This means that her parents do not speak to her. Marie's sister, a nursery nurse, has been living with her for a while, they get on well and she helps look after Jamie. But she was going for a job as a live-in nanny, so Marie and Jamie would soon be alone again.

'I blurted it out to my mum in a fit of crying. And she was all right about it. She said she would break the news to my dad. He didn't speak to me for ages. My mum said that he cried. But he avoided me. Even when I left home he wasn't speaking to me, and I'd been closer with him than with my mum. That's what hurts most now, because I don't see my dad. I was the oldest and he expected so much of me. Mum was really supportive, straightaway she started about the things we'd have to get, and going to the clinic and things.

Steve was a bit shocked. But then he was really pleased. It amazed me. Telling a bloke you've only known for a couple of months that you're pregnant. He went round telling all his family. He was over the moon, but his family weren't. His mother's never liked me. She thinks I'm too forward with people. She never thought I was good enough for her son. She always thought I trapped him, she thought I did it on purpose. Nobody brought up the subject of abortion. I'd never thought of getting pregnant, so I never thought of abortion. Of course Mum and Dad were against abortion anyway with their religion. But the doctor didn't even say. Looking back, I don't think I would have done.

I thought everything was going to be lovely. I was getting married. I lived in dreamland I suppose. You do when you're young. You don't think. I was four months pregnant when I got married. I wasn't big at all. I didn't get big till the last couple of months. I used to stick it out so that people would notice. I didn't think I'd be proud being a mum, but I was. I had to give up work a few months before.

I worked in a supermarket. Everyone said I was stupid getting married. Of course I was young and didn't believe any of it. Steve was due to go in to the army. So we thought if we got married before, we'd get a place.

He was only in the army four weeks. But he couldn't stand being away from me. And he doesn't like discipline. So he came out. Then I had Jamie. We lived in one room then. It was a big room, and we had our own bathroom and toilet, and kitchen. Steve was totally lazy. He used to like feeding Jamie, but nothing else. He thought a man goes out to earn money, and a wife stays at home. Even though he didn't have a job. We were stuck here together all day. We got on each other's nerves. We didn't have any money, so we couldn't go out in the evening either. It was all right to start with, but not after a while. Then things began to strain on him, and Jamie was crying all the time. So he couldn't cope any more, and he started taking it out on me. He saw a psychiatrist who said he couldn't take responsibility. He'd had such a bad upbringing that he was sent to a private school, because they didn't want him turning out like the rest of his family. He got loads of O and A levels but never did anything with them. He wanted to do what he wanted to do. So he had no job at all.

Then he started hitting me and that, for about seven or eight months. For no reason at all. It was either over something really petty, the TV or something, or nothing at all. At first I just sat there, but after a while I just legged it out the front door. But then he started on Jamie. So I left him. I saw my social worker and I had all bruises down my face. So she packed me in her car and drove me off. They put me in a battered wives home. But it was horrible there. All the other women were a lot older than me. I felt the odd one out. It was like a fortress. The only men allowed in were the solicitors. That's when I saw the solicitor and he started my divorce going. The first thing he did was to take my husband to court so I could get this place back. Then I'd moved back here two weeks, and I had a court order on him, and he came round here. He said he was going to commit suicide if I didn't take him back. I told him where the front door was. I'd had enough. I was thinking of Jamie now. It got to the stage where, as soon as my husband started hitting me, so would Jamie, he would come up and hit me too. He didn't know any different. But Steve would hit Jamie as well. That was the final thing. I could take it with me, but not with Jamie. I thought, because he'd seen a psychiatrist, I thought he could be helped. And because I thought I was in love with him, I thought I could help him. But when I tried to help, he thought I was interfering. He said, 'There's nothing wrong with me.' He said it was all my fault. It was a weird situation. But I don't feel about him the same way now.

When I first went to the doctor about my husband, I was given a social worker, but my husband didn't know. Nobody knew. And no one knew that he hit me. If I had bruises I'd stay in and not go out. I didn't want anybody to know. I felt ashamed. I thought it was my fault. It made me feel guilty. I'd never been married before so you don't really know what married life's like. When I first came back here it wasn't all right at first, because I was on my own. And Mum and Dad weren't talking to me because of the divorce. They knew by then that Steve had been hitting me. But they had a talk with the head of their religion and they said although I'm the daughter, it must be God or me. They chose God. I was hurt. I didn't know how they could do it. They were the only people I had in the world, and they deserted me. Mum had me before she got married. So it was the same for me as her really. I think she was twenty. None of her family would go to the wedding. Mum got thrown out, all her clothes chucked in the street for marrying a black man. They're all right with him now though. I think that's why she was so understanding when she found out I was pregnant. She'd been through it.

I came to love Jamie eventually. Still sometimes now I think, God I hate you. No, I love him really. Sometimes things just get on top of you. I couldn't love him at first, he was just a baby to me. Something to play with. Then when it came to the crying, I haven't got a lot of patience. I lose my temper easily. But I find it a lot easier to cope now, especially with my sister helping. If I didn't have her and was on my own with him, I'd still be stuck in all the time. And I wouldn't have had any affection for him at all. I haven't got any motherly instinct. But I've got to look after him. I liked the idea of having my own baby at first. It was lovely when he first came home from hospital because all he did was sleep. I can't wait till he's older, and we can talk together properly. It'll be better when he gets to school. I went to a playgroup, but I felt odd. They were all in their own little groups, and I just sat there. Jamie played, but he screamed at first, because he wanted all the toys to himself. As soon as we go out, he goes wild. I'd rather sit at home and have him play quietly. I'd thought of having him adopted, I was going to foster him with somebody. But I changed my mind. It was a couple of months after I split up with my husband. I was stuck in all the time. I thought it would always be like that. And Jamie played me and my sister against the other all the time. It was like he had two mums. He knows what he can get from my sister, and he knows what I'm like. He knows I'm not the affectionate type, so he goes to my sister for that. If he wants an argument, he comes to me. I hadn't actually signed anything, but it was going through. Then it hit me. I thought, I've had him all this time, what will I do when I don't have him. So I changed my mind.

When I'd just split up with my husband, and I had nobody to talk to, it was really hard. Plus getting back into the routine of boyfriends. I just wanted a bloke to care for me and look after me. But they'd use me. They'd sleep with me, and that was it. A couple did fall in love with me and wanted to marry me. But marriage scared me. No matter how I felt for them. Even if I liked them I didn't want marriage. But in a way I used them to start with because I'd got used to having sex regularly. But I'm still wary of men. One bloke, he was really nice. But as soon as he said he loved me, and wanted to marry me – as soon as he said that, well – I can't believe it when someone says that. So I end it then. It confuses people.

It's still hard not having my mum and dad to talk to. There's my sister, but it's not the same. I keep a lot of things to myself because there's nobody to tell. I put on a happy front all the time. Nobody knows me deep down. I wouldn't ever cry in front of anyone, no matter how I feel. I like to keep occupied, it stops me thinking, and I read a lot. I never have any money. We stay in every day. I am totally bored and get very depressed. The trouble is I can't see anything changing. It seems to me I'll always be stuck at home, never any money and I hate the thought of it. I want to work, travel, buy nice clothes and enjoy life. With a child this is impossible unless you marry a millionaire. That's why I've even tried suicide. I got really drunk one day and tried to cut my wrists.

When I was going to have Jamie adopted people said I was unloving and cruel but now I wish I had done it. One thing I would change about my past. I would never have had my son. I love him, I think I do anyway, but it has entirely ruined my life and I mean life. Kids are forever, that's what people don't realise. I think if you are happily married, have good parents who would help you whenever you needed it, if you had money, a nice home and a good future ahead of you, having children young is a lovely idea. But if you are single, you could be stuck in a bedsitter for years and no money. Trapped.

8
PERSONAL CHANGES

Becoming a mother blows apart the world that you've known. Life is never the same again. You are always responsible for someone else whose needs are more demanding and immediate than your own. It brings good things and bad things, and it takes some adapting to. When you are used to coming and going as you please, messing about, or being silly and irresponsible, being a mother brings you up with a jolt. One of the changes most often expressed by young mothers is how fast they had had to grow up. 'I was seventeen and a mother now,' said Mary. 'Having a baby so young made me grow up with bang.'

Growing up means putting someone else – your baby – first in your life. It means less or no time for yourself, little time or money to spend on clothes, records, make-up or social life. Your life is constrained and you can no longer be spontaneous. The very label 'teenage mother' implies a conflict in behaviour between being a teenager and a parent. Some young mothers find it hard to deal with this, although it is not always such a great loss.

> I feel confused. One minute I'm at a club dancing and being a normal young person, then I'm plunged back into being a mother. It's hard to adjust. You can't do anything without thinking of the baby first.   (Diane)

> I'm not confident like I used to be. Before I used to rush into things but now I think twice. My sister is still mad, doing crazy things, and I used to be like that. She says that I'm boring now like an old woman. But you can't act

like a sixteen-year-old when you've got a baby, can you?
(Debbie)

I know I am a mum but I don't know if I think of myself as one. I still like being a normal person as well, so I've got two different roles really. Sometimes I feel like being really silly, but I'm not supposed to do this. I'm supposed to be responsible, a mother, but I do like being a bit of a child sometimes. I've missed some things having Steven, but now I look at these young kids and think, I don't know how they can do that, hanging around the shops and that, dossing around, because I'm more grown up now. I can find better things to do with myself now.   (Bridget)

It often happens that I walk up the street and see girls my age dressed up to go out and all I do is housework. I take my son swimming and I want to play but I see other mothers being really sensible and then I feel silly.
(Claire)

Claire was committed to looking after her son and her husband. Joanne lives at home and takes minimal responsibility for her nine-month-old daughter because her mother enjoys taking over most of the childcare. Working by day and socialising at night, she feels she would go mad if she couldn't go out. Teresa also found it very hard to take responsibility for her baby at first, and took advantage of her mother being at home to go out like she used to before she was pregnant. It is only after three years that she has been able to come to terms with her role as a mother.

In becoming pregnant and having a baby, your social life is curtailed, and this may serve to show your true friends, who will stand by you and continue to give friendship and support. The way friends react to your pregnancy gives the first indication, and then whether they come and see you when you have to stay in looking after the baby. Melanie's friends live in a different area so only one of them comes up to see her and she doesn't stay very long: 'I don't think she knows what to talk about. I think I've changed. One girl said I'd gone awfully ignorant. I don't know why she thinks that.'

Diane's friends thought it was a novelty when she was first pregnant, but this wore off:

> There wasn't a day at first when I wasn't going out or someone was coming round. Then I stopped smoking and drinking. They also realised I wouldn't be able to form a foursome any more. So they knew I was no use in getting fixed up with boys. So they dropped me. If I 'phoned up and they weren't in they never 'phoned me back. I was generally regarded as a bore, even though I hadn't really changed at all. I was very unhappy and spent all my time alone except when I was with my family. Towards the end of my pregnancy Karen suddenly got interested again because the big event would soon happen. By this time I was so desperate for friends I welcomed her friendship. After I had Matthew she and I used to go out every weekend. Then she found some new friends and dropped me again. Now I've got some new friends and I don't bother any more.

Finding new friends may mean a particular sort of friend, one who is in a similar situation, as Lisa had found.

> I still see my old friends but I've got new ones as well. The thing is, we've got more in common because we've all got children. Sometimes when my old friends come up, things they talk about – boys – it's like they were still at school, I'm really just not interested in it.

This made Lisa feel old for her years, but rather than dropping her, her friends tended to use her as an 'agony aunt':

> Most of my friends, if they've got problems they'll come

to me. I was the first to know about my friend being pregnant, she came straight up to me. And some of my other friends do, even with silly things like both of them like the same boyfriend or something and they always think I've got all the answers. I feel bad because sometimes I think I might give them the wrong advice, but they'd rather come to me than their mums. I tend to think of what a mother would say now rather than a friend. That's the only thing, sometimes they don't get the advice they want, but they still come back for more.

Many of the positive changes that go with being a mother, at any age, are to do with the love and happiness that having a baby can bring – having a small child to kiss and cuddle, who responds and smiles, who loves you back and needs you. 'Having something of your very own that no one can take away.' Many feel proud to be mothers, proud of their beautiful babies. For a significant number of young mothers, having their baby has been the best thing that has happened to them, and they would not be without them.

Being a mother brings a role and status where there may have been none before. It can fill a need for love where this may have also been lacking. The bleak prospects that life on the dole offers many young women turn having a baby into the most fulfilling thing on the horizon, and gives them a reason for living. For those who have good educational prospects, a baby can also provide an added incentive to do something more with their lives than they might have done otherwise. Judy, for instance, felt that she had worked harder for her A-levels and put more into having a successful interview for her new job than she would have ever done without her eleven-month-old daughter. And Denise had been disillusioned with her further education course but now feels inspired by her tiny baby to do something with her life.

The most frequent complaints are about loss of freedom, feeling trapped, unable to do what you want, or to go where you want. Coming to terms with this is part of being a mother, but it can be very hard to do, especially if you are living on your own in a flat, without much money, without a job to go out to, no identity outside the home, and with few people to talk to. This is hard for all mothers, not just young ones. For those still living with their families, this situation is offset by having people around to talk to, who will usually take the baby for a while, babysit for the odd evening, and generally ease the stresses that can be involved. Wendy finds it lonely in her bleak council flat. Although she sees other young mothers during the day, she is on her own with the television every night after her daughter has gone to bed. Marie feels totally trapped in her flat with her son, is very depressed a lot of the time and often wishes that she never had him.

Being a teenage parent picks you out for attention, and being a single teenage parent even more so. All single parents tend to feel that they have to prove that they can cope as well as anyone else, and teenage mothers are no exception. One of the workers at a Young Mothers Project in Manchester specifically commented on this. She felt they were reluctant to leave their children in the creche provided because it had always been emphasised that it was their responsibility to care for their children. At first they also seemed to feel that people were watching them for ways in which they might be failing to be good mothers. This was also Cathy's experience.

My mum was always there if I needed her, but I always used to hear people saying, she'll soon get fed up and her mum will end up having the baby while she goes out. This used to make me feel quite mad, and made me determined to prove them wrong. I never go to discos or pubs. My mum says I am too possessive with her but I have to show them that I can do it, and now they all say, 'Isn't it good that she's turned out to be such a good little mum.' This makes me feel really good because I have proved that you don't have to be thirty years old to have a baby and have patience with children. You probably have more, and are a lot fitter to cope with all the getting up every night and early the next morning.

Regrets

Most young mothers are delighted with their babies. They are adamant that they don't regret having them, they would never wish them away, and they can no longer imagine what life would be like without them. However, there are quite a few things they would change if they could rerun their lives over again. While emphasising the benefits of having children when they are young, given a choice many would have preferred to wait until they were a bit older.

On reflection, many thought they had been naive, blind, or reckless about contraception. They wouldn't risk it again now. But at the time they went along with what was happening, it seemed unromantic or irrelevant to plan sex or worry about the consequences. Getting pregnant seemed very unreal and unlikely – something that happens to other people. Probably some of you reading this book think the same. It's easier to assume that the girls speaking here are different from you, and it won't happen. But they're not, and it might.

Invariably, another regret came from those who had delayed telling their parents they were pregnant. They were sorry for the hurt, worry and upset it had caused them. Most now realised this had been unnecessary although it was hard to see this at the time. It may have caused a temporary explosion but they would not have been chucked out, and ultimately their parents would have supported them. They also felt they had missed out by not being officially pregnant, and not being able to enjoy the status, recognition, and special attention that this brings. Some wished they could have proudly shown it off instead of guiltily holding themselves in and wearing baggy clothes.

Lost education was also mentioned, where pregnancy had put an instant end to qualifications or training, and it was difficult to see these being resumed in the near future. On the other hand, some of those who had little interest or ability at school or were regular truants before they got pregnant, have often positively benefitted by the personal teaching of the home tutoring system, or by the intense small group teaching in units such as the Arbour Project in Liverpool, and Barkerend in Bradford.

Some wished that they had had better experiences with men, especially when boyfriends had declared their love and support and then deserted them, or had proved to be irresponsible or cruel. Taking her daughter's father to court left Cathy and her family very bitter about him; and Nickie, trying to make ends meet alone in her bedsit, feels let down by her boyfriend who cannot take the responsibility of fatherhood, and gives her no help at all.

Despite these regrets, the positive aspects of being a teenage mother still shine through. It may not be the best time to have a baby, but it has its rewards, usually embodied in girls' close and loving relationships with their children, and watching them grow and develop. As always, it is more often the conditions of mothering – no money and inadequate housing – that put a strain on people and their relationships.

The teenage mothers talking in this book would re-organise many aspects of their personal histories if they could, but for many of them, what may have initially been a 'mistake', has transformed and enriched rather than ruined their lives.

TERESA

Teresa was a rebellious sixteen-year-old when she fell for her handsome boyfriend; he was her first real boyfriend and she thought he was the one. She neglected her schoolwork to go with him and his crowd, all much the same age as herself, and spent a lot of time hanging around drinking and glue-sniffing. She got pregnant as a result of just one occasion, shortly after which he went off with her friend. Still in love with him, and growing ever more pregnant, she became obsessed with watching them walk past her house down the road every night.

No one believed she was pregnant at first, because the break-up upset her so much she became anorexic and lost a lot of weight. Everyone thought she was just jealous and her friends were quite nasty to her. They eventually realised she was telling the truth. Her parents were very upset, especially as they are a Catholic family. Her father wouldn't speak to her for a week, and they have become less close as a result. But the family have given her a lot of help and support and it has brought her and her mother closer together.

After she had her son, Gary, things were all right for a while, but she could not adjust to being a mother. She wanted to go out and do the things she used to do, and she resented Gary for being there and stopping her. She still lived at home and left him in the care of her mother, whose ill health was not improved by her daughter's behaviour.

Finally, at the age of twenty, Teresa has realised what she has been doing and has come to terms with the situation. She even met up with Gary's father again and realised that she no longer felt the same about him. Her present boyfriend has helped her by making her feel that somebody cares, and has given her confidence. It has taken three years out of her life, but at last she feels capable of building a future for herself and her son.

'It started when I was sixteen, and as most teenagers I met a boy and fell hopelessly in love, or so I thought. In my case he was my first steady boyfriend and so everything was a new and exciting experience. I had just left school and was looking for a fulltime job. I had a Saturday job in a local supermarket. You could say I was just starting out in life and enjoying it too. When I met my boyfriend we just used to go to the pictures, parties, etc. And then we weren't on our own together, we were with our friends. We used to go around in a big group of boys and girls.

There really wasn't much to do at the time so we would just hang around the streets. But then the boys in the group started drinking and glue-sniffing and we would go with them. We used to spend most evenings just sitting in a nearby playing field where the boys would glue-sniff and the girls would drink. When I look back now I see how very stupid I was but at the time all that mattered was to be one of the crowd. I was very naive and the sort of easy led person, so I just followed the crowd. Then it became a craze and an obsession and we could not wait for the weekend just to buy a bottle of alcohol – gin, wine, etc., drink it, get drunk and have a laugh. It was then that I realised that at any cost and for any excuse this life was leading me to drink. I became very aggressive at home and my outlook on life was 'I don't care'. With the tension at home, my parents became worried and would tell me not to see my boyfriend. But I became bitter and just did the opposite of everything they told me.

My boyfriend, it seemed, was the only thing I had left. But at this time our relationship was coming to an end. So now it was my boyfriend who was my obsession and I would do anything to keep him. And so one night after too much to drink I did not need much persuasion to have sex with him, not thinking at the time of the consequences. I just felt loved, a feeling I desperately craved for. By now I was so much in love that I was blind to the fact that my boyfriend was seeing my best friend. After our relationship ended I found myself three months pregnant.

The experience of breaking up and being pregnant and not being able to tell anyone was too horrible to describe. I became very ill and wouldn't eat until finally I couldn't eat. I was so thin. And one day in a desperate plea for help I told my ex-boyfriend and of course he laughed in my face. As I had lost so much weight he couldn't see that I was three months pregnant so did not believe me. Eventually the news got round that I was lying just to get him back. So now I had no one, I was very scared and alone. Then things began to happen, when I went out I would find grafitti on the bus stops and walls about me. And then my neighbours began talking and watching me, so not only was I suffering but my parents as well. In the end I had to tell them, they were disgusted, shocked and very hurt. At about five months I regained my appetite and so the pregnancy showed a great deal. Now everyone saw I was not lying, and my ex-boyfriend was scared and denied being the father, which made me bitter and obsessed with trying to prove it.

It was a very long time before I accepted the fact that he would not be coming back and it was my responsibility. As I am a Catholic and have very strong views on abortion, that was out of the question, and I was too far gone. I was going to have the baby adopted but I changed my mind as soon as I saw my son. I felt now it was all over and my parents and family who had helped me through would not worry. Everything would be fine and we'd live happily ever after. The first year he was little and it was all lovely, people congratulate you and all this. The second year it was a pain to get up in the night to feed him.

The first two years were like a dream, and the crying got

to me a lot. It used to ring in my ears the whole time. It
used to send me mad. Gary's got a big pair of lungs, and he
just used to scream. It was just the little things that I wasn't
used to, that I thought would be nothing. They seemed to
be much more. There was a point about eighteen months
ago where I just couldn't stand it anymore. I had about two
weeks where I just rejected him, I couldn't stand to be near
him or anything. Anything I wanted to do, Gary came first.
So I began to blame him, also building inside a bitter
revenge for his father for leaving me to cope alone. A lot of
times I wanted to go out, and I'd creep around the room,
get ready and everything, and just as I went to go out the
door he'd wake up. And Mum would say, "No way." I used
to get so angry then.

Times were very hard it seemed. I would meet people
then tell them of my son and they would either walk away
so as not to get involved or turn away in disgust. I was very
aware of this wherever I went and so therefore lost self-
confidence and pride. You go out and think everyone is
talking about you. I've only just got rid of that. And we've
got some strange neighbours, they really did go overboard.
They started tying nappies to the gate, things like that.
I longed to be just like every other girl and have a good job
and a steady boyfriend. Instead I was waking up to a
screaming child, washing nappies, sleepless nights and
much more. I also longed for nice clothes and things that I
couldn't afford on DHSS money. And so it went on.

As Gary grew older life began to change at home. There
were constant arguments on what I was doing wrong and so
Gary became unbearable. In the end I pleaded with my
parents to look after him so I could go out to work. They
agreed and for a time it seemed to work. But finally
working very hard and coming home yet to work again and
look after Gary was too much. Also I couldn't take the guilt
of leaving Gary with my parents.

One half of me was so young, and the other half was trying to become mature and face up to responsibility. But you can't mix the both of them. I thought I could be two people at the same time. I thought I could be young and carefree, and have a baby. At first it was great, I was doing everything, nappies out on the line, up to the shop. But it got too much, so I started to go out. Mum looked after Gary. I thought he was young enough not to cause too much trouble. He was a good child, you'd put him to bed and he'd stay there. I thought she wouldn't have any trouble with him. So I'd go out. And it got later and later that I came home. I started going round with my friends again. I was slowly getting back to the way I was before. Going out, getting drunk. It was only, one night I came home and Mum said, "Right, I'm not feeding him tonight. If he wakes up you can feed him." And I was drunk. I'd gone to bed. I had a hangover, I had a headache, everything. The room was spinning. And he cried and I thought, oh no. I got up and had to feed him, and I fell asleep feeding him. When I woke up he wasn't there, and he wasn't in his cot. I went downstairs and Mum was sitting there feeding him. She said, "That's the last time." And it finally registered then. And I changed. I grew up a lot.

I've only just accepted that I'm a mother within the last couple of months. I went on holiday this year to sort myself out. And it did. I didn't think it would as much. I'd been out there for two days in Crete, and I was lying in the apartment one morning and a baby was crying and it woke me up. My friend was with me, and apparently I got out of bed and said, "All right, I'm coming." Then I woke up and thought, what am I doing? It's taught me a lot, good and bad. The bad is that I was so stupid. I was told to stop going around with the people I was with, but I didn't, because I thought I was going to end up with my boyfriend. I didn't think he'd go off with my best friend. But there's a lot of good come out of it. I've learned how much people do care about me. I thought nobody cared about me. I was a rebel myself, and the rebel in him, I thought nobody was like us, we were different. If I hadn't met my present boyfriend I may still have felt the same. He's helped a lot. He's made me know that somebody else does care, and somebody is willing to take Gary on.

I didn't want all this to happen to me. I used to see it happen to other girls at school, they used to get pregnant. I used to feel sorry for them. I thought I'd never like that to happen to me. We had endless family care lessons on it. We had films. One-parent families and what they go through, everything, so it's not as though I didn't know. But at the time you think, not me. I thought I had maternal instinct. But I didn't. I had to find it. When we had lessons at school, I was the most interested. I loved it. I felt I was really maternal, but I wasn't. When he cried, I didn't know what to do. My mum had to show me. And of course he'd go to her for a long time. He still does half the time. If he hurts himself he'll run and say, "Nanny". Not "Mummy". I'm torn between home life, I suppose part of me still wants to be with my parents, my parents' daughter, and part of me wants to be Gary's mother. You can't be both, but I've been obsessed with trying to prove it. It's made me feel I'm a failure, and I've been trying to prove I'm not. It's been hard and it's taken so long. It takes away your independence. That's what makes me angry. All I want now is just something to do to boost my confidence again. Independence. I really want that. When my boyfriend's friends say, "What do you do?", I think, don't ask that. I disappear to the toilet when I see they're getting around to it. I'm ashamed to say I work part-time behind a shop counter, at nearly twenty-one. When you've got it in you to want to do something, it makes you feel terrible. I love art. I'd like to do designing or something. I got grade 1 in art. I was doing well in school until the third year, then he came along and that was it.

I didn't know enough about sex. It was only what I picked up at school. I was stupid. I used to think you could get pregnant with heavy petting. Sometimes you can, but I thought you could definitely. I was having a period when I got pregnant. Just unlucky. I'd say to other girls, just be careful. I've read stories like my own and that's enough really. You learn from others' mistakes. There's so much I could say to others, but everyone's different. When you're that age, you won't take advice, but if you read my story and the troubles I've had. People want to know the effects, how to get themselves out of it, and it's not fair if you don't say.

Although I regret what I did I cannot say I regret keeping my son because as any mother I love him very much. But I would advise anyone in my or a similar situation to think carefully about motherhood. Because at the time it doesn't seem so bad when they are just tiny babies to care for but they don't stay babies forever. I have learnt the hard way that it is not easy to jump out of teenagehood into motherhood. It has taken nearly three years but I have the strength now to go on and make a better life for me and my son.

DENISE

Seventeen-year-old Denise is black and was born in London. Her parents come from South Africa, they split up when she was about ten-years-old. She quite enjoyed school until she was fourteen, but after that she couldn't wait to leave and do Art and Politics A-level at a college of further education, believing this would be different. But here she was disillusioned and felt she was not allowed to express her own views. Her parents had expected her to do well academically but she was not really interested.

When she discovered she was pregnant, she was shell-shocked. She couldn't face having an abortion, but having decided to keep the baby, she could not bring herself to tell anyone that she was pregnant. She couldn't tell her mother, who suffers from alcoholism, nor her white boyfriend, the father of the baby, although they were still seeing each other. She decided instead to make a fresh start, and put a pin in the map in a rural area miles away, which she had once visited and liked. Telling her family and friends she had got work down there, she left London. By this time she was six months pregnant. She initially found a tiny bedsit in a small country town. The only person from her previous life who knew of her predicament was her best friend.

When I spoke to Denise she was living in a small room with her eight-week old baby and managing on social security, plus some savings and birthday present money. Since then she has moved into a Mother and Baby Home, which she arranged for herself. She has also finally told her mother, who is planning to come down and visit her. Strongly determined to do her own thing, she appears very self-sufficient and together about her present situation and her plans for the future.

' A lot of people think that when you're young and have a baby, you're thick. Okay, it was a stupid mistake to make, it could have been avoided. But you're not stupid, just because of that. People tend to have that image of you. You've wasted your life, your youth, you're written off. If you read a magazine or hear something on the radio, people say they aren't going to ruin their lives having a baby. I don't think people plan to have kids when they're so young, I certainly didn't plan it that way. But it doesn't mean that's the end of your life. It's actually since she's been born that I've thought of doing more constructive things with my life. I was in a bit of a rut before, I was supposed to be doing my A-levels, but wasn't really interested, I wasn't motivated to do anything. Now I feel I want to do something with myself. She's given me a purpose in life really. Now I wake up to her smiling face in the mornings, and I feel I've got a reason to be here now. So I might as well do something with myself. Perhaps go back and finish my A-levels. Nothing definite yet, but something.

It sounds strange, but I went straight from home to down here, and the only person who asked if I was pregnant was her father. As far as I was concerned it was lucky, because I thought I'd be better off starting on my own. It's strange nobody knew about it, but I think I used to be quite sensible, and I think my mother trusted me. She said, "I knew Denise couldn't be pregnant because she would have told me." My sister had a little girl, but she couldn't cope with having a baby, and it went straight into a foster home. So at the back of my mind I had this feeling they would think I couldn't cope with my baby, so I thought it best not to tell them until I was settled.

My mum can be close and everything if everything's going fine. If things look a bit heavy and serious she tends to drift off. I don't think she feels she can quite handle it herself. So she pretends it's not there. That's why she didn't really notice I was pregnant. She told herself I wasn't. I wasn't that big actually. I've always worn quite baggy clothes. And it was winter. So I had loads of woollies. I told everybody I'd been bingeing and got a bit fat. I didn't tell Cherie's father because, although I think he cares about me, and I care very much for him, and we've known each other for quite a while, I didn't want him to think he had to marry me or something. Or move in with me. To give up everything because I was pregnant. I would have felt I'd trapped him. I thought it would be better if I could at least give myself a bit of breathing space. I wasn't very big till I was about six months, even then not very. I just looked fat. Someone made a comment about me, and my boyfriend asked me if I was pregnant, and I said no. He seemed angry. But I think it was because I wasn't telling him. Because I was being so secretive.

I don't know what his reaction would be now. I've no idea. If it was me, I wouldn't want someone to turn up and say, I've just had a baby. What do you do when all of a sudden there's a third person in your life you weren't expecting? We didn't have any thoughts of a permanent relationship. We just got on together and it went on and on. We split up a couple of times. It was fairly low-key. He did write to me. I've got myself in a really awkward position, I don't know how I'll get myself out of it. It's still down to me to say, I've had a baby. In a way I feel quite guilty, because I also think my mum would really enjoy her. I feel I'm depriving her.

At the time I just felt I couldn't have an abortion. I didn't know if I could look after a baby, but I thought I'll have the baby, and if there was any risk to her because I couldn't cope, I'd just have to have her adopted. I had to wait and see. I was looking forward to the worst of everything. Things turned out a lot better. I was petrified of pain. I was also petrified of being on my own. When it came to the birth, it wasn't frightening at all. I wasn't in control of what was happening, but I felt as though I was. Then looking after her, I thought she'd cry all the time and I wouldn't be able to do anything. Again, it wasn't that bad. The worst I thought it was going to be, the better it was and the more enjoyable. I suppose it could only be better than I'd feared.

I was lucky because, I went along to the first doctor I saw, and he put me in the hands of this midwife, who was wonderful, and basically looked after me. I've always been

181

lucky, you see. Which is why I do a lot of foolish things.
Like when I was having a sexual relationship without using
contraception. But if you are too lucky it makes you very
stupid. When I went with my friend to have a pregnancy
test, because we both thought we might be pregnant, I
thought I've been lucky so far. I thought then that if I was,
I would have an abortion. And if not, I'll go on the Pill.
Instead of that I had a baby.

When I actually started having a sexual relationship he
didn't really know it was only his idea. I let him think it was
mutual. Also, I let him think I was on the Pill, which is a
stupid thing. I don't know why. I don't like other people to
know my weaknesses. I knew it was irresponsible and that
it was a weakness, I intended to go on the Pill, so I thought
I'll tell him I'm on the Pill so he doesn't worry, and
everything will be all right. But I'm the same about
everything. I start out thinking, nothing serious is going to
come of this, and then if it does I think it's my fault because
I let it. So if there's anybody involved, I don't tell them.
When I became pregnant, I felt it wasn't my mother's
problem, it would only upset her. Why inflict it on her,
it's my fault. The same with my boyfriend, why worry him
with it. He hadn't done anything really, it was my fault.
Looking back, I think I should have talked it over with him.

I do miss her father. I think about him a lot, but I don't
know if I'll tell him. If I knew what he was thinking, how he
would feel, then it would be a lot easier for me. In a way I
think the longer I wait, the more unfair it will be for him.
And for her. Probably if I hadn't had her, we would have
still been together. I think the last thing that occurred to
him was to be a father. And me too, I suppose. I didn't even
like babies. So, I think in a way we were both too young to
take it on. We were unsure of ourselves and each other.
We started off as friends, you see. I don't think either of us
intended having a sexual relationship. I've thought about

if I opened the door and there he was. In a way I'd be delighted. In a way I'd be petrified. I just keep thinking to myself, if I were he, I'd be very annoyed. I feel I've conned him. About a lot of things. In his place I'd feel very cheated. Betrayed. So that makes me uncomfortable. But I still have this optimism, in spite of being foolish. Perhaps one of these days we'll get back together, and live happily ever after! It isn't very likely, but I can't help thinking it. But you see, I don't think I could live with him. I feel it would be rushed. But I do miss him a lot and think about him, and I would like to have more of his children.

Everyday now leaves me with a sense of achievement because my daughter's still alive and healthy, and although I'm not anything flash or clever, I feel special. It's great not being judged by exams or jobs, or things like that. I don't need anything like that to be judged by now, because I know I must be doing something right. Cherie's healthy and happy and everything. That's important to me, that I've done that. She seems quite pleased with what I do for her. It makes me think I'm somebody. It makes me feel good when people say she's lovely. It's nice feeling you haven't got to prove yourself. It's not an effort, but sometimes I feel I deserve congratulations.

When she was born she swallowed something nasty, and she had to go in a special care baby unit. So I had to be moved right after she was born. I was riding along in the ambulance, and I was tired, half asleep. I heard the midwife and the ambulance man chatting. He said to her something about me, and the midwife said, 'She'll be all right, she's got guts.' I felt great, it was nice to hear. If she thought I've got guts, I must do. It's good to think other people have confidence in you. I went to see the doctor once while I was pregnant and he made me feel very pathetic. Why didn't I go for any medical attention before, and that sort of thing. He made me feel really stupid. All right, so I had done something fairly stupid, but he made me feel like I didn't deserve to be alive. And that my child would just clutter up the world. I felt terrible after that. But when people have confidence in you, it gives you confidence in yourself. The last time I felt confident in myself was when I won a prize when I was about seven. Up till now I've always been somebody's daughter or somebody's pupil or whatever, and people always have this formula of you. They take you for whatever they've decided you are before they meet you. Now I'm just me.

It must be very difficult for girls like me who have babies who stay in the same place. People then expect them to be the same person but in another way they also expect them to behave differently. It's easier for me in that way. I just thought it was time I had a new beginning, with my new baby. And it has worked. I'm more confident now. I think I'm more tolerant. And a lot more easygoing. Like, if you ask how I organise my week – I don't. She organises it for me. I can't really put down plans. It's nice really. I always felt I ought to be doing something, working, or whatever, everything mapped out. But now, I don't have to be organised like that. I'm more flexible. I think I'm a much nicer person now. I like myself better. Obviously there are things you can't do when you've got a baby. But I don't think it has wasted my youth. You don't stop being young because you have a baby. And you don't stop being childish. Obviously you've got responsibilities, and you do change and you're more mature in that way. But you're also still the same person. So I have changed, but I haven't.

I think it's important to have confidence that you can do things for yourself. That you can change your life, and if you decide to have a baby, it will be your baby, and you're capable of bringing it up. But your life needn't end just because there's a baby in it. You can study, you can get a job if you want. You can go on living. That child isn't your

total existence. You can still have a life of your own. I think
a lot of girls don't realise that. They have it rammed down
their throats by their parents and teachers that now you've
got a baby you can't do anything else. You must be grown
up, you're not young any more. You're a mother now.
I think that's rubbish. Yes, you've responsibilities.
But you're still yourself. It doesn't make you inferior to
anyone else.

9

HAVING A DISABLED CHILD

Any pregnant woman has a small chance of giving birth to a disabled baby. It may be due to some inherited factor, or a chance combination of genes – such as if both partners are carriers of the cystic fibrosis gene. It may have to do with the particular conditions in the womb during pregnancy, or something that happens during a difficult delivery. Some abnormalities can be detected through early testing, such as Downs Syndrome (Mongolism) and spina bifida, which is why it is so important for pregnant women to go for regular antenatal check-ups from an early stage in their pregnancy. Other abnormalities defy medical prediction and are revealed only at birth, or some time afterwards, such as cystic fibrosis or cerebral palsy.

Since disabilities such as Downs Syndrome do not occur much in younger women, the test for these – amniocentisis – tends not to be given to women under thirty-five, unless there is some indication from early blood tests. Therefore it is not normally given to pregnant teenagers. This test also detects spina bifida. If such conditions are discovered early enough, the expectant mother may have the choice of an abortion, but if it's too late, she is at least prepared and can decide in advance whether to keep the baby or have it adopted at birth.

But it is not only older women who may have a severely disabled child, it can also happen to teenagers. If they decide to keep their baby, as some certainly do, their lives are even tougher and more constrained than other teenage mothers. Yet although it looks tragic from the outside, there may be something special and challenging about caring for such a child. I talked to two young mothers to whom this had happened. At the age of seven months, Lorraine's son was discovered to have cerebral palsy; and Debbie's daughter had been born with spina bifida and hydrocephalus (water on the brain).

LORRAINE

Lorraine is a cheerful blonde seventeen-year-old, living with her parents, two younger sisters and brother in a council house in the west of England. She was fourteen, still at school, and planning to train as a hairdresser when she became pregnant. It was many months before she and her mother realised this, and it came as a great surprise, since she had never had a period. By this time she was no longer with the baby's father, but with another boyfriend, who she still sees occasionally. At the time, neither the baby's teenage father nor his parents wished to have anything more to do with her or the baby, and although she often passes his house, it is as though they don't know each other.

Lorraine gave birth to Alex a few weeks prematurely, after a fairly short and easy birth. Her father was pleased it was a boy as he said this evened up the numbers in the family. Alex seemed a fine healthy baby, but after a few months they began to notice that something was not quite right, he didn't seem to be developing very fast, and at seven months he was diagnosed as being quite severely handicapped with cerebral palsy. Two parts of his brain are full of fluid and they will never heal up. He was also found to be deaf in one ear. At almost two years old he is very floppy and can hardly move around at all.

It came as a great shock at first, but Lorraine and the rest of her family have come to terms with it. At present

Lorraine and Alex are sharing a bedroom with Lorraine's two sisters, but the council is paying for an extra bedroom to be built on to the back of the house for them, on the condition that they stay there for another four years. The whole family loves and cares deeply for Alex, and work hard to stimulate him to develop as much as possible. He is very loving but extremely demanding and even with the invaluable support of her whole family, he has changed Lorraine's life even more than an ordinary baby.

'Alex's father had been the first serious boyfriend I'd ever been with, and I'd been going out with him for about four months. When he asked me to have sexual intercourse I said no, I didn't feel ready but he kept on and on one night and in the end I gave in. I was very on edge the whole time, but I never thought I could get pregnant. I thought that you could not get pregnant unless you had started your periods, but the doctor said the egg was there ready for my first period, and that was when it happened. Although I put on weight, because I was so slim it looked as though I was beginning to mature.

It was about six weeks before the summer holidays. My mum said I could do with losing some weight so we went to Keep Fit, which I couldn't keep up with and found it quite difficult to do some of the exercises. A few days later my mum asked if I was pregnant. She was worried because I'd started to put on weight much quicker. I was quite sure I wasn't but she kept on. She got me a pregnancy test and I did it one morning. It didn't take long to show it was positive. I was very shocked. I just can't put into words how I felt. I went up to the shop where my mum worked, and as soon as I walked through the doors my mum knew what the answer was. She took me to the doctor and he said I was seven months. When the doctor said this I just lay there thinking, Oh my God, I've only got eight weeks left.

The next thing was to tell my dad. My mum told him and then they came to pick me up. It must have been one of the most frightening things in my life having to face him. When I saw him we looked at each other and I just burst into tears and put my arms round him and said, "Sorry Dad". But he just said, "Don't worry, Lorraine, you're not the first and you're not the last." It was all right after that.

We suspected that Alex was a bit handicapped at three months. We never knew before. My dad kept saying, "There's something wrong with that baby." My boyfriend's mum noticed it as well, he had a virus, and a cough and he had this rash all over him. So I took him over the clinic, and the doctor there, she said it was only a cough. I didn't believe her, so to be on the safe side I went up my doctors. My doctor wasn't there, so this other doctor checked him over, and said it was only a virus, but said she wasn't very pleased about his head. It was a bit floppy, so they took him into hospital for tests. We knew then there was something wrong, but we didn't know what. At seven months they said he was handicapped. So then they started giving him physiotherapy. He has to have it most days, otherwise he tightens up. A physio used to come twice a week, but she stopped because of his nursery school, so then I did it, but now I haven't got so much time, so she's going to start again. They tried to do it in school, but his teachers don't know what to do. So we're trying to work hard on him at the moment. If he doesn't get it he just stiffens up and won't do anything. It loosens him up so that he can do things better. The looser he is the easier it is for him to move about. He does nothing at the moment. They're trying to get him to sit up by himself. We've got a standing frame which we put him in. He doesn't like that. He likes me holding him best.

When I found out he was handicapped, deep down I cared, but in front of my mum I didn't want to show that

I cared. So I hid it. My mum was upset, and when I saw her upset I didn't want to know, I would walk out or hide it. When it really hit me – and my boyfriend's mum came to the assessment with me – was when they said, "He's spastic." That horrible word. They said don't worry, it's just stiff muscles. There's nothing else wrong with him at all, his muscles are just stiff. The medical word is cerebral palsy. That's when it hit me. I got upset then. At the word spastic. I burst outside the room and started crying. My boyfriend's mum said, "I've worked with spastic children, and they are really clever." It was a bit better when she said that. But it was a shock. But now I know, I take it with a pinch of salt. Life goes on, doesn't it? We just have to try and work hard on him. They said he'll do it one day, but they don't know when. He's slow to pick up things, but once he's picked it up he'll do it all the time. We're working on his eyes at the moment. Keeping his eyes working.

We don't know what Alex is mentally yet until he starts doing things. Everything he does, we think, brilliant. It's nice when you see him do something. We just watch him all the time to see what he does. But it takes such a long time. He goes to a nursery now, it's a normal nursery, but part of it is for children with special needs. I take him, and I usually stay for about ten, fifteen minutes. Then I go to a friend's house, and I pick him up. I've only recently been able to do that, because he will not stay with anybody. Only me, and with my mum he will. It's quite hard work. If I take him out, it's moan, moan all the time. He doesn't like the push chair. And if we stop I have to take him out, I can't just leave him in it and chat to people or anything, I have to keep it moving. If I go to friends, I can't just leave him to play by himself, he has to sit on my lap all the time. He's very dependent on me at the moment. He's hard work really. Mum helps a lot. But it's best if he's with me mostly. Otherwise he wouldn't know who I was. Friday night is the only time I have my night out. I go into the town, to nightclubs and that. Other times, if I go up my boyfriend's, I take him with me. If I go to a pub, he comes with me. I take him everywhere with me. He sleeps with me. Since he was two weeks old I've had him with me. I tried him in his cot, but he won't go in it. But it's company for me in the night. Sometimes he pushes me out, and I end up on the floor.

Sometimes my boyfriend plays with him. Depends what mood he's in. But he's good about him really. Some boys wouldn't want to know. He accepts him. Sometimes he asks me questions like, when is he going to walk, and things. People do ask you that sometimes, and what can you say? I just say, he's got stiff muscles and he'll do it in his own time. But there's so many rumours that go round about him. Some say he's blind, or completely deaf, or never going to walk. Things like that. I try to forget that he is handicapped. But when people do say things like that, you have to say, well he's got stiff muscles and the doctors say he'll do it when he's ready. And they accept it then. Sometimes I get upset but I don't show it.

They say that Alex will walk but it will take ever such a long time. So that's what our target is. At first I thought, why me? Some of my friends have got kids and there's nothing wrong with them. And here's Alex, he's deaf and handicapped. But now, I just think I've got to accept it. I would have had an abortion if I'd known. I don't agree with them, but because I was so young then, and it is a tie, because I can't do what I want and I find it hard getting people to look after him. The hardest thing has been not being able to go out by myself. I can't go out without thinking I've got to be back at a certain time, if someone's looking after him. But they keep you company really. I don't have many people come to see me. But I'm quite happy sat at home. I do do Party Plan. Selling pottery, at parties. My mum has given me money, because it was sixteen before we could claim anything. Scrimping and scraping really. Because Alex has attacks, he'll get attendance allowance when he's two. Which is a bit of help. That's £30 a week. And I get extras for heating and laundry allowance as well. That's what I give to my mum for rent. Anything over that goes on the catalogue money. It's the only way I can afford clothes.

Alex looks just like a normal baby. You have to look really hard to know that there is anything wrong. But now I've got over the shock of him having cerebral palsy, I love his company even though he is very demanding and wants me by his side day and night. Looking back now, I am glad that I never got rid of him, but I do not wish it on any other young girl to keep a baby or even to mess about unless you are on the Pill or taking some sort of contraceptive because, believe me, it is very hard work looking after a child but even harder if they are handicapped. If I could go back, I'd make sure I never did it again. Take precautions. You always think it's never going to happen to you. Until it does. That's what I would advise, take precautions, and don't mess about. You can't really get people to realise that it's sensible to take precautions, I suppose. Maybe reading about them, they'd know then, what it involves.

LORRAINE'S MOTHER

When Lorraine's mother had become pregnant at seven-teen, her parents had forced her to have her baby son adopted. She still regrets this and wonders what happened to him. Two years later, she had Lorraine. She was there-fore very sympathetic to her daughter's plight, and there was no way that she was going to suggest adoption to her. It was she who first became suspicious about Lorraine and persuaded her to do a home pregnancy test. In retrospect, she, like Joanne's mother, was quite glad in some ways that she had not found out until so late about her daughter's pregnancy.

'We only had eight weeks to do everything. It was nice really because you didn't have time to think about it. We just got on with it. There wasn't a decision to make which I'm glad of, because I don't really like abortion. That would have been the most sensible thing. But as it was, she couldn't. There was no thought of adoption. But the decision was up to Lorraine, not to me. Looking back now, she was very young. She's grown up a lot these two years. But she's never been immature really. She's always been an "old" child. I had the twins when she was eighteen months, so she had to grow up rapidly. And she was surrounded by older people. It made her more independent than most children.

It's terrifying really how many girls are frightened of telling their parents. It happened to me. I was seventeen. It was dreadful. I stayed at somebody's house. My mum sussed me out in any case, she used to watch me like a hawk every month, you know. She kept on and on. I was two months. Well, you didn't have abortions then, only backstreet ones. And she told my dad. But the atmosphere was dreadful. I had no option but to have him adopted. That's why I feel so differently perhaps, because it happened to me. I had him for ten days in hospital, and then I had to give him up. It was dreadful. I had to buy him all his clothes. I was booked for a Mother and Baby Home. That frightened me to death. It was the first time I'd been away from home. I thought, six weeks away with the baby, whatever's going to happen? When I was in hospital for the ten days I just went to pieces.

It's enough to have a baby, then to think of other things as well, it's too much. The last day I fed him, and I knew he was going, it was dreadful. I put a barrier up. Every time I fed him I used to think, I can't keep you. I couldn't give him any love because I knew I couldn't keep him. It was an awful experience. When he was three months, it was the official adoption papers, and it really hit me then that he didn't belong to me. Never. He's nineteen now. Sometimes I think perhaps, God willing, he might want to find me. It would be nice. I wasn't as fortunate as Lorraine, I couldn't keep him. So it must have influenced how I felt then, and I did say it was entirely up to her, whatever she chose to do.

She wanted me with her at the birth, and I knew that if I was going to be with her, I wouldn't be able to let him go. But I knew my daughter. I knew she wouldn't. So he belongs to us. He's your own flesh and blood. You can't give them up. I think it's cruel to expect someone to do it, really. My parents wouldn't let me have a choice. They didn't even go in and see him.

It was ever so strange telling her dad. I came back and said, "I think you'd better sit down, I've got something to tell you." And he thought our Peter had burnt down the dairy, because that had just been burnt down. I said "I don't know whether it's worse or better than that. Lorraine's pregnant." He just sat there. He got up and washed his hands and said, "I must be the youngest grandfather going." We were thirty-five. He never criticised her, or run her down. He was really good. Alex's father said the best thing was to have it adopted. But I said, it's my grandchild. And it's theirs, as well, whether they like it or not. But he paid his way. He pays his bit, whatever it is. The Social sort that out. He's got away with it lightly.

Lorraine had him in the August. That was quite something. I thought it would never happen. I was at work and they rang from the clinic and said she was halfway gone. I ran up there. And she looked so upset. My heart went out to her. I knew exactly what she was going through. And she was so young. The sister said to me, she needs you now. She had problems with pushing and he got stuck. His face was lying the other way. They had to twist him. I'm glad I was there. I didn't know whether I'd find enough strength. But I'm glad I was there. I wouldn't have missed it for anything. When he came out! Oh. He was like a little boxer. Screwed up. He wanted to be fed straightway. She had no drugs or anything. She was so brave.

As the weeks went by I thought there was something strange about Alex, although I couldn't see anything wrong with him. I couldn't understand why he cried so much and he wouldn't sleep or settle. We got quite despaired. So we took him to the clinic in the afternoon and the doctor wasn't at all happy. She admitted him to hospital that afternoon. Because of his head. He wasn't keeping his head up. Then at seven months they said he was handicapped. By nine months they said he was spastic, which is cerebral palsy. You don't think about it until it happens to you. I didn't even think he was handicapped. It was a shock really. But it doesn't matter any more, all those feelings have gone. You just get on with it. I never felt bitter towards anybody. It was just something that happened. I just felt so sorry for Alex. And for Lorraine. I wondered what kind of a life would be in front of her. But she wanted to keep him and she was worried that they'd take him away. They're going to introduce a foster family soon, so that if Lorraine wants to go away or anything, or go out, he'll get to know them and be happy with them. It'll give us all a break. Because you can't just leave him. You can't leave him for a minute.

It's lucky really that we're quite a large family. It would have been awful if Lorraine had been an only child. With so many of us in the house, it takes it off. Always someone around him. But he's more of a pleasure now he's better. You get a reaction now. The two years have gone quite quickly really. A tough two years. It did put a strain on me.

I got very anxious. I felt anxious for Lorraine. How can fifteen-year-olds know what to do with a small baby? She knew nothing about babies. A little tomboy. I felt I had to show her how to do things, make things, show her it all. There again, she had been taught things, in the hospital. A bit different to how I did them. But I always said, I wanted him to be her baby. I wanted him to know who his mum was. At first I felt I had to have very broad shoulders, I felt thoroughly responsible for the pair of them. But she doesn't need me so much now. She can cope now. Now and again I come home from work at lunchtime and I can see she's had enough. So I just take him off her for an hour. She doesn't get dressed usually till I come in, because she can't get a shower or anything without him screaming and crying. I couldn't cope with another baby. I couldn't stand it. But Alex is not mine. As much as I love him, he's not mine. When I look after him on Friday nights, and put him upstairs, I think, thank God for that.

The reactions from my mother – oh, my God, it was dreadful. It was like the end of the world to her. I went and told her, and she said, "Of course you'll have it adopted, won't you." I said no. She went through a phase that people were ignoring her in the street, and talking about her. That's how it affected her. But I'm afraid I have no sympathy. We had a big argument because of the years I've been through, all my pent up feelings about what I went through came out. I couldn't say anything at the time, I was so young, and frightened. So it all came out then. She ended up in tears. But I just got it all off my chest, after all those years. Everybody was upset about Alex, obviously. But when you sit down and think about it, it's not the end of the world.

DEBBIE

Debbie is twenty, with curly blonde hair, and lives with her little daughter Jennie in a council house on an estate in a Midlands city. She was eighteen when she got pregnant. Having been pressurised into having an abortion by her mother six months earlier, she was determined to have this one and kept quiet about it. She was about eight months pregnant when it was discovered that her baby had spina bifida and would probably die. However, Jennie lived and so far has defied all such predictions. Although she has no movement from the waist down and will never walk, she is cheerful, intelligent and pretty, and Debbie is optimistically looking towards her second birthday.

As well as spina bifida, Jennie has hydrocephalus, (water on the brain), which is often associated with this condition. She has had several operations, one of which inserted a valve to drain the fluid off into her stomach. Debbie has had to give her constant care and attention, initially dressing the open wound in her back, a well as the normal activities of feeding and changing her every few hours.

Jennie's father, who is black, was nineteen when she was born, and had originally been pleased at the idea of being a father, but he is ashamed that his daughter is handicapped. He and Debbie lived in a flat together from when she was pregnant until Jennie was about a year old, but it did not work out. When she got her council house a few months previously, he did not move in with her and the relationship ended.

Debbie's mother herself got pregnant at sixteen, which is why she was so adamant about Debbie's abortion, and she too had a spina bifida baby, but it died. Given her medical history, it was very unfortunate that the baby's condition was not detected until too late in the pregnancy. Both parents have been very supportive and are proud that she has coped so well.

Jennie is very hard work but Debbie loves her and there is no way she would give her up. There is a strong bond between them and she feels she has met the challenge of looking after her. It is never clear how long children with spina bifida will live, and every week that goes by is a bonus.

'I had quite a difficult pregnancy. I fainted a few times, I was anaemic and when I was seven-and-a-half months gone I was rushed into hospital because I was bleeding. I was made to rest completely for a week or else I would have lost the baby. But if I'd known that the baby would be disabled I wouldn't have bothered. I didn't bother going to antenatal classes, but obviously I went to the antenatal clinic. It was there that I was told that the baby was spina bifida and she would definitely be born dead or die a few hours after birth. I was about eight months at this time and I was asked if I wanted to be induced to save it dragging on any longer, and I said no. When I was told the baby would not live, I took everything back to the shops, the pushchair, cots, etc. The hardest thing was telling my boyfriend about the baby, he cried and I felt a failure. In the end I persuaded myself that it was all for the best and planned a future out for myself after I'd had the baby. I was going to get a job, learn to drive and me and my boyfriend were going to get married.

Despite all the problems I enjoyed the pregnancy. I felt special. The best part about being pregnant is that you can eat and eat because you're only going to get fatter and fatter anyway. I thought my boyfriend would be embarrassed or ashamed to walk down the road with me but he wasn't. In the last month or so I got really depressed. I couldn't wait until it was all over and done with and I could get back to going out and partying. I also got very bitter because I thought, "Well, I'm going through all this and it's not even going to be worth it."

I was warned I'd have a difficult birth, and I did! I went into labour at 3.15 one morning and Jennie finally arrived at 7.24 the following morning. Because she had hydrocephalus, her head was too large to pass through due to the excess fluid on her brain, so I had to be cut and forceps were used, then I had to be stitched up again. This was absolute agony afterwards. I remember spending New Year's Eve lying on a bag of ice to try and soothe my stitches.

As soon as she was born Jennie was taken to the Special Care Baby Unit and literally left in a corner until she was to die. I was taken to see her in the afternoon and my mum and dad were there holding her. She was so tiny, I'd never seen a new-born baby before. The first thing I noticed were her blue eyes, which half-caste babies don't usually have. They're still blue now. She's beautiful! When I saw her on the next morning I went mad because the nurses weren't bothering with her. The doctors gave me the choice of taking her home or leaving her in the hospital to die. They were sure she was going to die. First they said she would die at birth and when she lived they only gave her two or three days. Then they said six months and now they're saying two years.

When I was in hospital the nurses were showing all the others who'd had babies how to look after them and bath them. I couldn't do anything like that. I could only sponge her down because of the hole in her back. They had to teach me how to do her dressings. At three months she had an operation to close it up. When she was first born she didn't move. It's only been the last year or two that she's been moving like this. She's doing lots of things now that the doctors said she shouldn't be doing. And she's been talking for a while. She's proved every doctor wrong so far.

When I used to see people that I knew, I used to think, why me and not them? If I had found out what she was going to be like when I was three or four months pregnant then I would have had it terminated. Sometimes, I do think that it would have been better if she had died at birth. She's happy at the moment but when she gets older she's going to look at the other children playing and she's going to ask why she can't walk. I don't think about the responsibility. It frightens me to think about it. When she was first born she was just like any other baby. Now that she's getting older it's going to get harder and harder on me looking after her. She's good as gold though. She never cries.

Up until Jennie was about six months I wouldn't have worried if she had died because I didn't want her. Because I thought she was going to die I didn't love her and didn't let myself get attached to her. I just acted like a nurse looking after a patient. Then after six months when she got stronger, I changed, I wouldn't part with her. If she does die it will be upsetting when you think that I've looked after her every day for nearly two years. The doctors say that she's come on so well because she's loved by me and my family. I used to spoil her a lot when she was a baby but I try not to spoil her so much now. My mother and dad still spoil her. When she was born I didn't have anything for her. I didn't have any money. My mother and father took me to the shops and bought everything for her. Anything that she needs they get for her, but I feel guilty. From now on, if I want anything, I'm going to save up and get it myself. But I only have £43 a week on social security, and by the time I've paid my gas and electricity and everything and food I've got nothing left. By about Friday or Saturday my food's run out and I'm starving. On Sunday I go to my mum's and just eat all day and that lasts me all the week.

It's really tiring looking after Jennie, but not so much

now that I don't have to feed her every four hours like when she was a baby. Then I was feeding her, changing her nappy and her dressing at the same time all through the night and it was freezing cold. My boyfriend just used to turn over and go fast asleep, and leave me to it. He never had the patience to feed her. He never changed her nappy, he said he couldn't do it. It just gets routine in the end and you don't know whether it's day or night. She was about three months old when we moved into the flat. The weather was very cold, it snowed. I wouldn't take her out, I wanted to watch her chest. I stayed in for days on end. I got very tired in the end and I looked terrible. My whole life revolved around her. I just did it. She was mine and I had to look after her. Sometimes I still feel guilty for bringing her into the world. She's got two things against her. First she's half-caste and then she's disabled. When I go up to town with her some people say, oh, she's a bit darker than you. People say that she's a lovely colour, just look at her dark skin.

Having Jennie affected my relationship with my boyfriend. He said he wished she'd died at birth. He's ashamed of her. He'd never walk out in the street when I was pushing her. I don't know if it was his attitude towards her that broke it up. His relationship with me completely changed. He was all right when I was in the hospital but it changed when I came out. I couldn't believe the change in him. He stayed out most of the time and got involved with a young girl. He beat me up twice and the doctor at the hospital saw my bruises and I still stuck up for him. I said that I'd walked into a door. The next time that he beat me up and the doctor saw my bruises he said that if it happened again Jennie would have to be taken into care. Because my baby was born disabled I tried even harder to look after her and I know now I pushed out my boyfriend and I know it made him jealous and this put a strain on our relationship.

We split up three months ago. He still loves me, he says, but he broke my nose two weeks ago. If he can't have me then no one else is going to have me. I'm going to court next week to get an injunction. I'm bitter that he's out there leading the life that he had before I had Jennie. He's just as free as he was. And I'm here scrimping each week, looking after his child. I want him to hate her so that he won't bother with her.

Before I had her my father and I didn't get on at all. I had to leave home. When I was pregnant he didn't talk to me, but when I had her and he came to see me it was different. Now we get on fine. And he cares for Jennie so much. He's helped me out too much during the last eighteen months. I can't argue with him now. My relationship with my mother is much the same but I listen to her more now. When she gives me advice I sit down and think about it and realise that she's right. Both my parents help me a lot, emotionally and financially. I know now that they didn't mean what they said when they first found out I was pregnant. They don't treat me like a child now. I know they're very worried about me. My father wants me to go back home but their house isn't big enough. Anyway I'm happy enough on my own – although I never thought I would be!

When she was born I felt that I was forced to look after her. The doctors said, you're her mother and you must look after her. My mum and dad said that I had to do everything for her myself. It's done me good really because if they had taken over I wouldn't have bothered with her. I was determined that I would bring her up good. If it kills me I'll look after her. Sometimes I just wish I could have a couple of days to myself to do what I wanted. But I can't.

I always said that I didn't want a baby until I was about twenty-six. If I could start again and go back to being sixteen I would get a career either in clerical work or modelling, save enough money and start off married life properly, that is, in our own house and being able to pay the bills, and *then* think of having babies. I don't think babies should be brought up by only one parent, a baby needs a mother and a father.

I'd say to any other girls that having a baby isn't as easy and straightforward as it seems. Anything can happen to a baby whilst it is developing in the womb, as I found out! Also I'd tell them that a baby won't necessarily bring you and your boyfriend closer together. Everyone knows teenage boys aren't as mature as girls and they just can't handle the responsibility and you're left on your own. There's plenty of time in the future for you to have babies.

Although Jennie is disabled, she's just as clever as other babies, in fact the doctors have said she's forward for her age, but when anyone is told she's disabled they expect something to be mentally wrong with her as well. They say, "Oh, isn't she beautiful, you wouldn't think there is anything wrong with her." I've been asked why I haven't given her up for adoption so I can carry on with modelling, but they just don't understand that I love her so much. I couldn't possibly let anyone take her away from me.'

10

ALTERNATIVES –
ADOPTION AND ABORTION

Three options face you as a pregnant teenager – adoption, abortion, or keeping the baby. Up until the 1960s, adoption was a fairly common course of action for single pregnant teenagers, especially for those from better-off or professional backgrounds. But times were changing, and the broadening of attitudes towards sexuality, together with the easing of the law on abortion in 1968 made adoption an increasingly less popular choice, and today the total number of children put up for adoption is low. Being young and unmarried with a baby is not so unusual nowadays, and has lost much of its social stigma. If you definitely do not want a child, it has also become a lot easier and cheaper to terminate a pregnancy than in the past. Most teenagers today see only two visible alternatives – having a baby or having an abortion – but a few do still have their babies adopted.

Adoption

When, not so long ago, negative social attitudes towards teenage pregnancy and illegitimacy made it much harder to contemplate keeping your baby, adoption was often the only solution. Nowadays it has become a minority option taken up by those who don't want a baby but are too late to have their pregnancy terminated. In some cases this is a very straightforward choice, but for others it is hard to go through a pregnancy and birth and then give the baby away. Some girls spend their pregnancy assuming that they will have their baby adopted, either through their own choice, or by parental persuasion. Two of the young mothers I spoke to had done this, but had changed their minds as soon as their babies were born. Teresa, who had had her three-year-old son when she was seventeen, was one of these:

I was having him adopted right up to the minute he was born. Then they made the mistake of letting me see him. Mind you, I might have asked to see him anyway, or the suspense would have killed me for the rest of my life. They didn't realise till he was born, that the couple of minutes it took me to see him that was it. I could see his dad in him, I could see me in him. It felt I'd known him all my life, the face was so familiar. Lovely little baby. I said, 'That's it. I want him.' The adoption woman came round and she just said, 'Congratulations!' Nobody had told her. After, I said, 'How did you know?' and she said, 'From the look on your face.'

Vickie too had arranged for an adoption. Pregnant at fifteen, her boyfriend 'had a fit and didn't want to know', so she just shut it out of her mind, hoping it would disappear. She was still at school, and got very skilful at wearing baggy clothes. She concealed it until she was six-and-a-half months, when her mother asked her if she was pregnant, and she had to reluctantly admit it. Her mother never spoke to her for the rest of her pregnancy and her father 'wasn't too pleasant either'. They gave her little support and she felt that her social worker was the only person who could understand. When visitors came to her home she was banished upstairs and not allowed to be seen:

I was going to give the baby up for adoption but I still wanted to look after her while I was in hospital. Anyway, after a long labour I gave birth to a beautiful, bouncy baby girl. I was overjoyed. They gave her to me and I felt that I never wanted to give her up. My mother was with me then. I already had a name for her, Sophie; so she's called that. I felt like I wanted to stay in hospital forever just so I could keep her. After four days my social worker said she'd have to take her so I just broke down and said that I wanted to keep her. She said I'd have to discuss it with my parents. When I did, they didn't seem too happy over the fact but they said they couldn't force me either way. The social worker had to take her away from me for a few days as I had nothing for her. That was on my sixteenth birthday. We bought things for her and people gave me clothes, etc. I would say that I was very lucky. Then I went to get her back and I was so proud.

Although Teresa had a hard time adjusting to mother-hood, neither she nor Vickie regret keeping their babies. But some mothers do experience doubts, especially if life becomes hard and lonely and they are very depressed. Marie had considered having her three-year-old son fostered, and Yvonne now wonders if she wouldn't have been better off if her daughter had been adopted, as planned.

SHEILA

For Sheila, living in Scotland, there was no change of heart when her daughter was born and adopted six years ago. It was the choice of both her and her parents and she has no regrets. She was sixteen when her boyfriend raped her, and she didn't see him again. He does not even know that he made her pregnant and that she had a baby. No one knew at that time, because she became very ill with glandular fever and it was not realised until she was well on in the pregnancy. There was never any question of her keeping the baby, and she went to a Mother and Baby Home before and after the birth. From there she went back to school, took her exams and went to art college to carry on with her life. Her parents were in the process of splitting up when this happened, and she now lives with her mother with whom her pregnancy is still a very sensitive subject. It was her second boyfriend and her first sexual experience, and this has affected her subsequent relationships. Fortunately she has now found a steady boyfriend who knows and understands how she feels.

'I didn't realise I was pregnant until I was seven months because I was in bed ill for three months with glandular fever. I lost a lot of weight instead of putting it on, I went down to six stone, 'cos I wasn't eating at all, I couldn't keep anything down. The doctors were visiting me every day and examining me and they didn't even realise I was pregnant, so I've lost all faith in doctors and hospitals as well through that. Also my parents were in the process of splitting up at the time and they were very wrapped up in themselves and I don't think they realised – they just sort of left me to get on with my life and I was supposed to be getting on with sitting my highers at school and studying for them and no one was particularly interested in that. My mum was very angry with me. My dad was just shocked. I suppose in his way he was more supportive than my mum, more sensible. My mum still feels like that, and sometimes when we have arguments I know that that's what's bugging her in the back of her mind. It doesn't bother me now though.

I realise how naive I was then. I wish I could have stood up for myself more, not in the sense that I wanted to keep the baby, but just the way I was treated. I was really left on my own to think things out for myself all the time, and I was too young to think things out, too young to realise what was going on, so that's why I was packed away to a mother and baby home. For me it was decided there and then, as soon as they found out, that it would be adopted, and a week later I was taken to this home and I was there until a week after I had the baby. It just seemed as if there was no other alternative. I didn't want the baby. My life would've been hell if I'd had it really, so there was no other alternative. It was the only way really to keep it quiet, 'cos I couldn't really live at home. It was me that suggested it because I don't think they knew what to do so they asked the doctor and the doctor found out about one and that was that – I didn't like it at the time but – I was in amongst about twenty girls all in the same position, and we could all sit and talk about it and laugh about it, and support each other. A lot of them ended up keeping their babies, about five out of the twenty didn't, a lot of them changed their minds to keep it.

I never saw the father again. I didn't want anything to do with him at the time. I was only sixteen when I was going out with him. I didn't want to sleep with him but he did and that was that. He was five years older than me. I was so naive I didn't really realise what had actually happened, I mean I knew what he'd done but I didn't realise the extent of the damage until I thought back on it. But I was sitting in the home and was thinking of it and generated a lot of hate towards him, hate that I never realised I could have, but it doesn't bother me now.

On the night it happened, my parents weren't in when I got home, and I had no one to talk to. I just went straight to my bed because I didn't feel well. My parents weren't very approachable anyway, I couldn't talk to them about things like that, so I just never told them, and the days went by and it just got harder and harder to say it, so when I knew I was pregnant and I tried to explain how it happened, they didn't believe me. And when I tried to explain it as well they just didn't want to listen, they were just too busy thinking about the fact in hand, of what to do about it.

I've thought it all out over six years and it doesn't really bother me now. Well, it does sometimes. I used to think the world of my parents and then as you get older you realise that they're not perfect; at that time they were very wrapped up in themselves; it was a year later that they split up. They were both very bitter towards each other and they used me to sort of foist their anger about each other. They didn't realise what they were doing and when I tried to tell them, they wouldn't admit it.

I was immediately referred to a social worker, but she wasn't really any help. She was an older woman and she retired while she was dealing with my case. Then, with the adoption papers six weeks after the birth, it was a different social worker, she was quite a nice lady, but it felt like all these strangers dealing with something that was meant to be extremely private. I just wanted to get rid of it and get on with my life, and I felt angry towards guys. And I felt so guilty because my parents made me feel guilty when they came to visit me. When they left I always used to be in tears. I don't see why I should have felt like that at all, but they always made me feel like that. I suppose it was a good thing being in that home amongst the other girls because they were all feeling the same sort of thing. It was run by nuns, it was Catholic. My family are Protestant, but it was just that there were only two homes in the area.

I hated being pregnant, it was sort of dictating my life I couldn't go off and do what I wanted to do and so I had to sit and wait and wait. It didn't really feel like a baby, but it gave me a shock every now and then, and I thought yes it is a baby, and obviously when it was kicking and things like that. In the home we were all really quite scared but we wouldn't admit it to each other, just sort of joke about it, which was good, good that we had each other, we were all really good friends. I kept in touch with one girl, but you shouldn't, its sad 'cos nobody really wanted to keep in touch but yet you did, as we all got on so well. But if you wanted to get on with your life you really had to make that break, block it out of your life, but I did keep in touch with one girl, she's since married and got divorced, and she's younger than me. She had hers adopted too.

The birth was quite painful but I was just so happy that that was it, and I just wanted to get back home and get on with things. I didn't get to sit my highers, obviously. I went back to the home. Then I had to go back after six weeks for the postnatal. I never saw the baby. I never really wanted to see her. I was just curious to know that she was all right, you know, normal. But after the birth the nurses were very off-hand, they weren't really interested in me. They had to keep me in the antenatal ward, even though I wasn't pregnant, they couldn't put me in the postnatal ward because there were babies there, so they kept me in a room off the ward, because all the nurses didn't realise I wasn't pregnant, and they used to wonder why I was lying on my stomach and things like that, and make funny remarks, and wonder why the bed was all blood and things like that. I really was very tired afterwards and I couldn't be bothered to tell them, if they wanted to find out they could.

I had to give her a name and register her as soon as I came out of hospital. I gave her the name Karen, but the adoptive parents can change it to anything they like. I've still got the birth certificate, but I've just got a wee copy, the proper one was given to the parents. They're not allowed to tell you about who had adopted her. The only thing they're allowed to do is if there's anything special you want – like if you think she might be interested in art, – ask to give her every chance you can, but there's nothing really I wanted in particular. I sometimes feel curious about her; I wouldn't be normal if I didn't. I wonder because I was so ill, up till I was about six or seven months pregnant – it could easily have harmed her. I don't know if

they would tell you if she wasn't normal. I suppose it's
better just not to know. If you think about it too much it
does get you down, but afterwards I just wanted to prove to
my parents that I was sensible and just ready to get on with
sitting my Highers and things like that, I didn't really let
it get me down at the time. I just came home and applied to
college and did my Highers there and did a Diploma
course after that, in Art and Design, and I specialised in
graphics, that's what I'd wanted to do. I did what I'd have
done if I'd never have got pregnant. Art has always come
first in my life, every aspect of it.

I only really went out with three different people since
that happened. Two of them were really very casual men,
but the guy I'm going out with now I've been going out
with for five years, and he knows all about it, I told him
everything, he was great, really understanding. I couldn't
believe it. I still can't believe how nice he is. I still don't
trust him really. I treat him pretty badly really because of
that, because I still think, well you're a guy and that's the
way all guys are, but it's not. I wouldn't let him near me at
first. The fact that I'm still living with my mother and yet
I've been going out with him for years I think says a lot.
I mean I could have easily been married and had about
three children by now if it weren't for that. All my friends
are getting married and some are divorced by now. He
keeps saying why don't we get engaged but it's not what I
want. I've got to convince myself that I can be completely
independent first.

I think abortion should be there for any women to make
the choice, but in that respect I don't regret the birth, I've
made a childless couple happy. I don't mean I'd like to have
a baby just for that, but I don't think, if only I'd had an
abortion, because it wasn't her fault. If I had known earlier
it would probably have been quite easy to make the
decision because I was very young, and I think I would

have been totally pressurised into it by my parents. Looking back I wish it had never happened, I wish I'd never met the guy, that's the biggest regret in my life. But I don't feel any pangs of regret about the adoption. The only thing is if she tries to find me when she's eighteen I don't know what I'm going to say to her. That she was born out of love, conceived out of love like everybody dreams that they were. But I think most people who do that have some kind of preconceived dream in their mind of a rich, beautiful . . . 'some sort of romantic story behind it.

Abortion

Abortion is a complex issue, and one about which a lot of people have very strong moral and emotional views, as did most of the mothers in this book. Many suggested that their disapproval of abortion was a factor influencing their decision to continue their pregnancy. Some, who were too many months pregnant to have an abortion, declared looking back that they would not have had one in any case. This may well be true, and they are now very committed to being mothers, but you don't always know exactly how you are going to feel until you are faced with the decision, and for many other girls, abortion still remains the best solution to an unintended and unwanted pregnancy.

A lot of girls have abortions every year. Figures show that between 1970 and 1980, the number of teenagers in England and Wales having abortions rose from 15,000 to 36,000, with a levelling off in the mid-1970s. (Figures are lower in Scotland.) This follows the implementation of the Abortion Act in 1968, and also reflects the change in teenage attitudes to pregnancy over this time. Previously it was something that had to be accepted with passive resignation, as it was not so easy to either prevent pregnancy effectively or to terminate it.

Girls who choose to terminate their pregnancies do so

for a number of reasons. Maybe they are very young; or they are not in a stable relationship and cannot face the prospect of bringing up a child alone; or they are unwilling to give up their education and career aspirations; or it may simply be that the pregnancy was unintended and a baby would be unwelcome at this stage in their lives. Sometimes girls are also pressured into abortions by their parents, doctors or boyfriends.

Returning to her girls' school after having her baby, Folasade was amazed to discover how many other girls had had abortions. 'Before it was, why me? Nobody else gets pregnant. Then I found out lots of people have got pregnant, they just had abortions. Sure you can have the baby if you want, but the most practical way would be not to have it. So you have an abortion.'

The decision may depend as much on a girl's circumstances as on her personality, and also what is acceptable within her family and culture. Proportionally more pregnant teenagers from middle-class backgrounds have abortions than those from working-class backgrounds, in which it is more usual and acceptable to get pregnant at a young age, continue the pregnancy and get married. This is also reflected in studies of attitudes to abortion, one of which showed that more middle-class girls than working-class girls approve of abortion. It found that over half of all girls said that they personally would either never consider abortion, or only on strong medical grounds.[1] Attitudes and behaviour do not always go so closely together, and if a girl actually does become pregnant her decision may not match her original attitudes. Views may change too as girls get older, when the romanticism surrounding the image of motherhood may be seen in a more practical perspective.

Denise believes that it is every woman's right to have an abortion, if that's what she feels is best. She used to think that if she got pregnant before her mid or late twenties,

213

she would have an abortion. But when she got pregnant, she felt differently:

> Now I don't think I could ever have one. Even when I wasn't sure I was pregnant, I felt there was something alive in me, it was weird, really different. When I got pregnant it felt like an irreversible state. I mean, if I'd had an abortion I'd still have *been* pregnant. All sorts of things happen to you but that really did seem irreversible to me. I remember one girl at school who got pregnant when she was fourteen and had an abortion. She just went back to school. I thought, how could you do it? I respect her for getting on with her life, but I don't think I could have done it myself. Pretending that nothing had ever happened. I thought, rather than trying to do that, I'd face up to having a baby and try and get on with my life rather than trying to go back. At the time I just felt I couldn't have an abortion. I didn't know if I could look after a baby, but I thought I'll have the baby, and if there was any risk to her because I couldn't cope I'd just have to have her adopted.

The best and safest time to have an abortion is within the first twelve weeks, when it is done by vacuum aspiration with few risks. The majority of 16–19-year-olds have these. The others have later abortions, which may partly be because of their own delay in recognising their pregnancy and making it known, but also because of delays in hospital appointments and referrals. Although getting an abortion is much easier than in the past, the cutbacks in the National Health Service nowadays slow down the process and cause unnecessary distress. Because Vickie's appointment with the hospital took so long, she had to have a private abortion, which is obviously expensive. (Abortions are free on the NHS.) After twelve weeks, abortions are usually done by inducing labour, which is a less simple process and carries more risks.

On the whole, research shows that teenagers cope well psychologically with abortion, and that longterm effects are fairly rare. However, it does suggest that they may be more prone to shortterm feelings of distress and guilt. Having an abortion may not take long, but it is very different psychologically to an operation to take out a tooth. It is a deeper loss than that, and you may feel very sad as a result, even if you have definitely not wanted a baby and are relieved not to be pregnant anymore. Mourning such a loss is to be expected, but there is no set reaction, and some girls have abortions without such an emotional response. The crucial factor is to allow anyone who is pregnant to make up their own minds. They should have access to good counselling that provides information, time and support so that they can decide for themselves and take responsibility for whatever course of action they choose. Pressuring people is the worst thing to do, and this probably produces the most lasting negative effects.

In Folasade's view, having a baby may be the more passive solution:

> I think people who have abortions are a lot stronger than people who don't. People who have the baby don't have to make the decision, they just sit there and do nothing. People who have an abortion make the decision, they have to have it done, and they have to live with it. Nobody else can help them, it's down to them.

Six months after Vickie changed her mind over adoption and brought her baby daughter back from hospital, she found another boyfriend who seemed to love her daughter, and with whom she had a wonderful time. They were using contraceptives but she got pregnant again.

> He didn't want to know, so I had to face telling my parents again and I decided I'd have an abortion, but

I had to go private because of my doctor messing me around. It took me three or four weeks to get an appointment down at the hospital. By then it was too late. So I had to go down to Brighton to have it. I made his parents pay half and as I had money in the bank I had to use that. I didn't cope very well with it, and for months afterwards I went through a very deep depression and I kept telling myself that I'd killed my baby. I have got over that as best as I ever will.

Vickie had made her own decision to have an abortion when she got pregnant a second time, but she still found it quite hard to come to terms with it afterwards. Tracy also became pregnant a second time through a contraceptive failure, but having been pressured into having a baby by her boyfriend, she was determined to make up her own mind this time.

After I had Sally, I didn't want another one. I panicked when my period was late. My mum went mad. I told her I didn't want to keep it. My boyfriend was upset, he wanted to keep it. This time I thought, why should I do what they want, I did that last time and look what happened, although I wouldn't dream of taking it out on her now. But why should I have to go through it again? This boyfriend wasn't as dominant as the other one, so I said I didn't want it. He threatened to leave but I said it made no difference, even though I like him. I didn't tell my dad though, or anybody else. I felt ashamed of having an abortion. I don't know why. I didn't plan to get pregnant. They say Durex is 99 per cent reliable. I suppose I was the unlucky one.

I don't know why I felt differently from the first time. In a way I did want the baby, but then I didn't. I didn't think about it after. My boyfriend used to say, it would be so old by now if you'd kept it, that sort of thing, and my sister-in-law was a bit off towards me, saying I'd killed a baby. I didn't think of it like that. It was a relief in a way. I'm not depressed now, either. It hasn't bothered me. This time I felt differently. My mum suggested an abortion the first time and I couldn't. I wasn't anti-abortion. I suppose I just followed him through, he was so domineering. Perhaps I wanted something to love of my own.

If girls have abortions against their will, or have them with insufficient thought or counselling, they may experience a lot of guilt and regret afterwards. The only way to compensate for this may then be to get pregnant again as soon as possible, and whether they do this purposely or not, they feel strongly that they don't want to have an abortion this time. Debbie had been pressured into an abortion by her parents six months before she had her daughter, and it had upset her a lot:

My mother and father forced me to have it. She took me to the family planning clinic and said that if I didn't sign then I wouldn't be allowed to go home that night. I said okay and then I went back in and signed the forms. Two days later I had the abortion. It was the most horrible thing in the world. I was just ten weeks pregnant. If I had been a bit further on I said to my mum, would you still have made me have it? She said 'yes'. I was only seventeen and she said I was too young. She didn't want me to have the kind of life she had. She wanted me to get somewhere, and she didn't like him because he was black. When I got pregnant again I hid it from her, but she knew. That's when I left home. They asked me if I was going to get rid of this one as well and I said 'no'.

It is very important that good and sensitive counselling is available for anyone considering an abortion. This means having someone to talk to about your pregnancy, your situation and how you feel about it all, who will explain your various alternatives, and help you to work out the most appropriate course of action for you. This should not involve pressuring you or telling you what to do. Ultimately the decision should be yours. The best sources of counselling in Britain are places such as the Brooke Advisory Centres, and the Pregnancy Advisory Service,[2] where staff have been specially trained. Individual social workers and other professionals may be helpful, but they may not present things in the most appropriate way.

Just as good news does make the newspapers, so there are usually more reports of people for whom an abortion has been an upsetting and stressful experience. It can be an experience that girls and women still find very hard to express their feelings about. Clearly, having an abortion can be a very ambivalent event,[3] but many girls do deal with it in a very straightforward way, and return to their lives with perhaps relief in the knowledge that this was essentially the right thing for them and what they wanted. At this stage in their lives, having a baby could have been a disaster, or at least something that would have changed the course of their lives in a depressing rather than an uplifting way. A pregnant woman carries the responsibility for two lives, not only that of a potential baby, but her own future life too, and that is very important to consider.'

11
LOOKING BACK – REFLECTIONS OF OLDER TEENAGE MOTHERS

It often seems as though the way you are feeling at the time will last forever. If you are feeling wonderfully happy and life couldn't be more perfect, it is difficult to imagine a day when you will not feel this way. If you are feeling low and depressed and nothing good has happened, it's hard to see how life will change. For better or for worse, life does change, and people change too.

Most of the young mothers talking here are still in their teens, their children are small, and they are immersed in the joys of babyhood and the challenging problems of immediate survival. Their baby is usually the most important thing in their lives and every day is taken as it comes. As the years go by and children get older and start going to school, there is more time for reflection. Many things have happened by this time. For some young mothers life has worked out very happily, but for many it is a continual struggle for survival. This is caused by poor conditions of housing, and trying to live on Social Security and other benefits. The nature of everyday life also varies according to where they live and who they live with, and how well this is working out. If they have ended up alone with their children, this may have its advantages, as many will testify, but it can be lonely.

With the passing of years, it is possible to test out the hope expressed by many young mothers that they will be closer to their children through having them at a young age. As I said earlier, this may not always happen. as girls and boys in their teens are often trying to separate themselves from their parents in order to find their own self identities, and this can stand in the way of shared confidences. However, it serves as a positive and optimistic justification for having children at the time. For Margaret, who had her daughter sixteen years ago when she was seventeen, it has proved to be true.

I'm glad I was young when I had her. It is like two people sharing a house. We are friends, we go on shopping trips together and try on clothes. When I asked her if she was worried about being seen out shopping with her mum she said that I had a young outlook, I wasn't old, so it was okay.

When Margaret had her daughter, unmarried teenage mothers had a certain notoriety. She had subsequently married her daughter's father, although the marriage later broke up. It was only recently that she had ever spoken to her daughter about the history of her birth.

She said she knew. I didn't ask how she knew, I tried to explain, through tears, how much I'd loved her dad. It was very painful for me although I can talk to strangers openly about it. I managed to tell her that every year, until this year, on her birthday, I've thought about another girl who was born that day in the same hospital as she was. She was the result of a holiday romance and her mother put her up for adoption. I was adamant I was keeping my baby. On her birthday I always wondered whether I had done the right thing or whether I was selfish, if I should have had her adopted, as she's not had a wonderful life. Her father, after I married him, became an alcoholic and the marriage ended violently and she is now the child of a divorced family. But funnily, this year on her birthday, her sixteenth, I didn't ask the question. I knew I'd made the right choice. I was at peace with myself at last.

It is sometimes very hard to know if you have made the right decisions in life, and with time you may begin to think about things you may have missed, such as opportunities to study, work or travel, which are often drastically curtailed with pregnancy. At the time, there seems to be lots of years left in which to do other things, and by the time the children are more independent, teenage mothers hope they will still be able to return to education or pursue other activities. Once the first few demanding years of babyhood have passed and children start school, mothers of any age often have a strong desire to do something to give them a separate sense of identity, independence and self-confidence.[1] This may involve getting a job, especially if money is tight, or taking a course in something. Going back to college is not impossible, as Kate demonstrated by getting her A-levels and going to university.

The three teenage mothers telling their stories here – Mary, Yvonne and Rosemary – are now in their twenties. They look back over their lives since they had their children.

MARY

Mary became pregnant at sixteen. She was working in the factory where she met Ian, the father of her eight-year-old son Paul. Ian was her first real boyfriend and they lived for the moment. When she told her parents she was pregnant, her mother was annoyed at first, but did get used to the idea. Her father's attitude was very reassuring until he found out she was not going to have an abortion, when he became very cold with her for the rest of her pregnancy.

Mary and the baby lived with her parents at first and

later together with Ian in a flat, but the relationship deteriorated and finally ended. Ian was one year older than Mary, and he could not face the responsibilities involved or handle the lack of money. Mary had support from her parents, and she and her father became particularly close after her mother died. She is proud of her son and wouldn't be without him, but she spent some very lonely times and it took a long time before she was ready to face another relationship with anyone.

'The first few months of pregnancy were hard. I had morning sickness and felt pretty awful sometimes. I felt so guilty and I felt I'd let everyone down. I didn't like being at home so I went round to Ian's all the time. I pleaded with him to ask his mum if we could sleep together but his mum wouldn't allow it. I was already pregnant so it couldn't have done any harm. I was so scared and desperately needed someone to hold me and tell me everything would be okay and the one time I really needed Ian with me the most it wasn't allowed and I cried myself to sleep.

After this the fuss died down a bit and it got easier. I quite enjoyed being pregnant. I looked good and I felt good. Me and Ian had our ups-and-downs but basically he was very good. He gave his mum some money each week to save for when we needed to buy things for the baby, though I do remember when the time came he was a bit reluctant to part with it all and didn't seem too thrilled at spending his money on nappies, a cot and a pram.

I was blissfully unaware of what would happen at the birth. I didn't realise what I'd have to go through and I wasn't too worried about it. The actual birth was terrible. I didn't know what to expect and no one had really told me. I've never been so petrified in my whole life and I wanted someone, but my mum was at home and Ian had been told to go into the waiting-room. I screamed and cried all the way through the birth. In the end the doctor had to cut me and use forceps to drag the baby out. It was a nightmare. I had no idea it would ever be so bad. I was so relieved it was all over and my baby was all right and I held him for the first time.

When we came home, Ian was still living with his parents and me and Paul were living with my mum and dad. Things were still a little bit frosty between me and my dad, but when I came home from the hospital I asked him to hold Paul. From then on my dad was wonderful to both me and the baby. I was extremely lucky, both my mum and dad were great and helped me so much. I honestly don't think I'd have managed so well without them. Ian came round most evenings to see us. I was very happy. All the unpleasantness of before was over and everyone loved Paul and I was so proud of him. I was very happy at home. Paul was as good as gold and I enjoyed looking after him. We didn't have very much money, but enough to get by and I never felt that I was missing out in any way. Then when Paul was about four months I was offered a flat.

The idea of moving into a home of my own did not scare me a bit, but I knew it was too good a chance to miss. I thought Ian would be delighted that we would all be together, but he wasn't too sure at first. But I was seventeen and a mother now. Having a baby so young made me grow up with a bang. Having a flat of our own was a novelty and we quite enjoyed it to start with. Some evenings a couple of Ian's friends would come round and we had some laughs.

It was like that for a year or so and then it changed. The novelty wore off a bit and Ian's friends came round less and less. Most nights it was just me and Ian and he was usually pretty tired after being at work all day long. Money was always a problem. Ian didn't earn much and after we'd paid the bills and bought food for the week there wasn't much left over. We stared to row over stupid things and then didn't talk properly for days.

There was never enough money. I wanted my bills paid on time and Ian was fed up of working hard and never having any money to spend on himself. I tried to talk to him but he didn't want to know and he'd just stare at the telly and I'd get more and more annoyed with him. I was beginning to hate him and I dreaded him coming home from work each night. Then Ian lost his job and we had even less money and I was worried sick we were going to lose the flat. Everything seemed to go wrong and it was one argument after another.

I couldn't take it anymore. It was getting too much for both of us and we were getting nowhere. I asked Ian to go before we both said things we'd really regret. I felt awful about it, but I knew it was the right thing to do. Everything had happened too quickly for us, having the flat was more difficult than either of us had ever imagined it would be.

Ian went back to live with his mum and dad. The next few months on my own were so hard. The days weren't too bad, I had Paul to see to, and things to do in the flat. But the nights were the worst. Every evening I'd put Paul to bed about six o'clock and then I was all on my own. I'd just watch the telly, or play some records. I desperately wanted to talk to someone, and I prayed someone would come round but no one ever did. I felt so lonely. It was absolute hell and it lasted for about six months. To this day I don't know how I got through it.

Eventually things started to get a bit easier. I got used to being on my own and I tried to do things in the evenings so I wouldn't get so fed up. I started seeing Ian again a few months after we'd split up. He sometimes came round to see me and Paul for an hour or two. He would've liked us to get back together again but I couldn't. We'd been through so much over the last few years and it just wasn't the same any more. I'd changed. I wasn't the same person as I'd been when we first met.

Then suddenly things started to look up. One day I went downstairs to answer the doorbell and it was two old friends, Mike and Colin. They were both out of work and had decided to try a window cleaning round and were looking for customers. They started to pop round to see me. It was so lovely to have someone to talk to again. Then an old school friend of mine came round to see me and asked if I'd like to go out with her and her friend one evening. It was great. For the first time in months I was beginning to feel happy again. Most nights I was still on my own and I still got a bit miserable, but it was a lot easier now I had some friends. Mum and Dad were very pleased and encouraged me to go, and my dad would come round and babysit.

Now I was able to go out occasionally, I started to meet blokes. It was very flattering if anyone showed a bit of interest in me but I didn't really want to get involved with a bloke and I tried not to encourage them in any way. I didn't want a boyfriend. I still hadn't got over everything that had happened with me and Ian and I didn't want to walk straight into another relationship. I had to think about Paul too. He was my life and anyone who wanted me would have to love him too. Love me, love my son.

Unfortunately when Paul was only three years old my mum died. I think it helped my dad a lot having me and Paul around. Because I was still living on my own, I could see my dad every single day. We had lunch together and me and Paul went round to Sunday dinner. My dad still encouraged me to go out with my friends and he'd babysit for Paul whenever I wanted. I wish now that I'd made more of an effort to do some of the things for myself and hadn't always turned to my dad for help every time. Perhaps then my dad wouldn't get so hurt when I want to do things on my own sometimes.

It's been very hard sometimes but I've managed to cope. Actually it annoys me, I always seem to bloody cope and I don't know why. People tend to think that it couldn't have been that bad, when all the time it was literally tearing you apart. We have our ups-and-downs and Paul annoys me sometimes but on the whole we get on really well. I'm very proud of him, and I'm quite proud of myself for bringing him up.

I'm still living on my own, but I do go out quite a bit and I've got friends who come round and see me. I do get fed up with the flat sometimes, all the cooking and cleaning and having to try and juggle the money each week so I can pay the bills. I'm not very good with money so it's not that easy and I do get into a bit of a mess at times. I'm on Supplementary Benefits but it's only just enough to get by. There isn't enough to buy nice clothes for me and Paul and do the things you'd really like to do. But my dad has always been there to help me out. Sometimes I feel guilty that we had to rely on him so much, and it isn't really fair.

I've got a boyfriend now. I've known him a long time and we've always been very good friends and he's taken me out sometimes. But it's only just recently that I've felt I was ready to take a chance and go out with someone proper. He knows all about me and Paul and Ian so I haven't had to explain too much to him. I can be quite awkward at times and I get quite moody for no real reason, but he tries to be patient with me.

Basically I'm quite happy with my life now. We have our problems, and I get pretty fed up and wonder what's going to happen to me and Paul in the future, I just don't know so I suppose I'll just have to muddle through each day and do the best I can.

YVONNE

For Yvonne, life has been a chapter of misfortunes. At fifteen she met her daughter's father in the supermarket where they both worked. Eddie was a month younger than her. She was working there for the summer before going to college for a year, after which she hoped to join the army. Unlike the others, she got little parental support when she was pregnant and was put in a mother and baby home. She was stuck in the middle between her dominating father who wanted her to have the baby adopted, and her boyfriend, who was threatening her if she did not keep it. After seven years of ups and downs in which she had relatively little support from anyone, she is still lonely and depressed, and can't help wishing that she had opted for adoption.

'It was a disaster from the beginning. My father is a very religious man, we are Roman Catholic and as soon as he found out that Eddie was Church of England he took and instant dislike to him. He said I was never to see Eddie again and how could I think of going out with someone from a different religious background. Of course I carried on seeing him. I started missing college, lying about where I was going, until I was eventually seen in a pub with him which got back to my dad. Mum was very much on my side but didn't want to get involved, so she used to sit and cry while Dad and I sat arguing.

That Christmas was terrible. On New Year's Eve I went to a party, telling my mum I was staying at my friend's house. Actually Eddie had arranged for me to stop at his house. I don't remember the party or anything that happened afterwards, but when I woke the next morning, Eddie told me that he had finally managed to persuade me to let him go all the way. In previous weeks I'd gone as far as getting in bed with him and we had attempted it a few

227

times but I was too scared.

In the weeks that followed I started feeling sick in the mornings and my back really ached, but it never occurred to me I might be pregnant. By the end of February, I was no longer attending college and found myself a job. My dad by this time had given up speaking to me, so he never knew whether I was still seeing Eddie or not.

At the beginning of May I had a pregnancy test and it was positive, Eddie said we would have to get married. I said no way was I going to get married and be saddled with a kid. I carried on going to work in my jeans and changed when I got there. I was under the illusion that if I didn't talk about it, it would go away.

Then my mum said it was about time I went on a diet as I was putting on a lot of weight. I went bright red and walked away. The next morning the hospital appointment card came. My mum recognised the code on the envelope from when she had worked there so she knew what it was. She flew upstairs and went mad. She said I had to have an abortion. By this time I was five months so that suggestion was a waste of time.

When I came home from work Mum carted me off to see the priest and before I knew what was happening I was in a home for unmarried mothers run by nuns. I spent three days there, then my parents came to collect me. It had been arranged that Eddie and his parents came round that night, and my dad just went completely over the top. He wanted to know where it happened, when it had happened, how many times we had done it, had we enjoyed it – I have never felt so humiliated in all my life. Then he calmed down, told Eddie he was never to come near me again, and that he had arranged for me to go into a home, have the baby adopted, come home and return to work. All of this I knew nothing about.

I carried on working till the end of the month, during

which I celebrated my seventeenth birthday. Then I was sent to the home, where we were made to scrub floors, clean toilets and weed the gardens. We were allowed few visitors and had to go to church every day. One day while out for a walk I met Eddie. He said he'd been waiting to see me for weeks and threatened that if I had the baby adopted he'd never leave me alone and he'd tell everyone what I'd done. I was really frightened.

In September with ten days to go, his parents came to see me to persuade me to keep the baby, saying that Eddie loved me and wanted to marry me. Three days later I saw him and said I would keep the baby if that was what he wanted. I went back to the home and the following afternoon I gave birth to my daughter, Cheryl. I remember feeling nothing at the time, I just kept telling myself thank God it's all over. My parents knew but they never came near, and later I found out that my mum had wanted to come and see me but my dad forbade her.

I felt nothing towards the baby. I fed her, changed her and slept for five days until I was discharged. I went back to the home for a fortnight and then I was moved into a homeless families unit. I had a letter from my mum telling me it wasn't too late to change my mind that I could still have her adopted and go home, but Eddie kept threatening me and I was so frightened that I never replied.

I used to get up at six, feed Cheryl, do the jobs that I'd been allocated, go to his parents till 9.30 at night, then come back and go to bed. His mum used to look after the baby while I slept all day. This went on until December when I decided I'd had enough. On Christmas Eve I packed my bags, picked up the baby and walked out. I rang my auntie and uncle, told them everything and sat in the park until they came to collect me. My uncle took me home where my mum broke down, my dad wouldn't even look at me. We survived Christmas, and Eddie and I got engaged.

I now spent half the week at home and the rest of the time with Eddie and his parents. After my eighteenth birthday things started to go wrong. He lost his job, started pinching my money and knocking me about but I stayed with him, because he said if I didn't he would put my mum's windows through. I made a clean break with Eddie after he beat me up for the last time. For weeks he sat outside my parents' house waiting for them to go to work, then if I went out he would follow me and shout abuse and tell people I was a slag or a bitch.

Soon after, I moved into a council house and for the first time I was on my own with my daughter. By this time Cheryl was nineteen months old and had started to talk. I felt really good. A week before my nineteenth birthday she found a box of matches downstairs and set fire to the settee. Within minutes the whole house was ablaze, and we escaped by jumping out of the bedroom window. The house was gutted and we lost everything. I stayed at my parents for a week and then the council offered me another house in the same street.

I started decorating the house and building my life again and things were going well for once. Cheryl started playschool, she made friends with some of the children and I made friends with their mothers. I celebrated my twenty-first birthday and around that time I made friends with my neighbour's fifteen-year-old daughter. She had a young sister who started to play with Cheryl. We had a really good summer, playing tennis, taking the children to the park, and just sitting talking until the early hours of the morning. It was as though I was recapturing my lost youth.

When my friend returned to school I really missed her. My daughter started nursery and I just used to go to school, do the shopping and the rest of the time I spent indoors, it was like I was afraid to go out. During the holidays Cheryl and I would go out for days, go shopping and visiting and then she would return to school and the feelings of not wanting to go out would return.

I never spoke to anyone about it because I felt really silly. I had a good relationship with my mum and my dad was speaking to me. I never went out at night, in fact I had hardly been out since Cheryl was born. When Cheryl started fulltime school I became really low and depressed.

A few months ago I got a job at a chip shop near me on Friday, Saturday and Sunday nights. Cheryl spent the weekends with my parents and at first it was really good. Then the summer holidays came and I was so used to being on my own that I resented having to find things for Cheryl to do. We went away to stay with some other cousins for two weeks and had a good time. I was really envious of them, because they were younger than me and had no ties or responsibilities. We went out at night and Cheryl stayed with my cousin's wife's mother and never once did I feel guilty about this. I was enjoying myself too much.

Once we came home and school started, I was and am back to feeling depressed again. I have started doing typing and book-keeping two mornings a week. I have my job, a nice house, a few good friends. I get on well with my parents now, my little girl is well-behaved, well-dressed, well-mannered – in fact, she is all you could wish for. Yet if I could turn the clock back eight years I would, and I would definitely opt for adoption. I'm not saying I don't love her, because I do, but I feel that everything I want to do, she is in the way of. So to those who say they wouldn't swap their babies, let them see how they feel in five years time when their children start school and the real loneliness sets in.

Cheryl still sees her father, a fact that I resent because he now has someone else, while I'm left all alone. Once she has gone to bed at 8.30, I chain and bolt the door, and am often in bed at nine o'clock myself. At twenty-four I feel too young to be among the other mothers, yet too old for people of my own age who are working and getting on with their lives. I also regret that I never finished my education, and that I never joined the army.

I would say to anyone who finds themselves in the situation I did, think very hard, eighteen years of your life is a lot to devote to a child, when you're still only a child yourself.'

ROSEMARY

For Rosemary, life has worked out quite well. Pregnant at sixteen, she left school instead of taking her A-levels and married the father of her baby. Her eldest son was born a few months later. She and her husband are still together eleven years later, have two more children and she has begun her education again.

'I was starting the sixth form at school. I had done well in my O-levels and I was expected to do well in my A-levels. I had met my husband during the summer holidays. He is a year older than me, had left school and was working. We came from totally different social backgounds. I came from a "typical" middle-class home, where there was just me and one sister. He is the eldest of five children, in a "typical" working-class family.

At the time I definitely feel I was in a bit of a "rut" in my life. I had been at school for years, a lot of my friends had left and I was fed up. I knew the risks I was taking in not using proper precautions but at the time it was a risk I was prepared to take. We were both rather shy with each other and it was something we were rather embarrassed to talk about. Neither of us had really been able to talk freely about sex with our parents, something we often reflect on now, and so we just practised the withdrawal method which, of course, is totally unreliable.

When I look back it is hard to remember exactly how I felt when I thought I was pregnant. I know I was scared, but that was knowing I had to tell my parents. I felt I'd let them down, and that is something I still feel guilty about even now. It was much easier for my husband to tell his parents, and they took it much more easily than mine did. Now I can see why that was but at the time I couldn't really understand. Within my husband's family, to marry and have your children young is quite a normal thing to do. Both his mother and grandmother were married at sixteen, although his mum was twenty before she had her first child. They also didn't have particularly high expectations for my husband careerwise. He had a relatively secure job, the money wasn't too bad and the fact that he was going to marry and have a child wasn't going to change that. They were shocked, of course, when he first told them, but they were definitely able to accept it more easily than my parents did.

My mum and dad probably had high expectations of me, something I can only really understand now that I have children of my own. They probably had their own plans for me to take my A-levels, go to university or college, then a good job before settling down to marriage and babies. It really must have been a great disappointment to them. It is still quite hard for me to talk or write about this. I feel really guilty that I let them down. My dad died nearly two years ago and I know he was proud of his three grandsons but I would have liked him to see that I was attempting to do something with my life now. I think it took a long time for him to come to terms with the fact that I was having a baby and getting married. He wasn't the kind of man who really showed his true feelings and I realise that it must have been a very difficult time for him, as it was for me. It is said that men are very protective towards their daughters and I'm sure this was definitely the case with us.

I remember breaking down and telling my mum I thought I was pregnant, but I think she'd already guessed. I couldn't tell my dad, she had to do that for me. Telling my boyfriend was much easier, he was shocked of course, but pleased as well, and very keen to get married as soon as possible. His parents were all for this, and very keen to help us and support us. My parents were rather harder to persuade. First of all they tried to persuade me to have an abortion but that was a non-starter. I knew that I was going to have my baby and keep it. Then they said that I could have the baby and stay at home with their support but not get married until I was sure that was what I wanted. However, at the time I was determined that I was going to get married before the baby was born. His parents backed us up, offering us a home until we could get one of our own.

I left school at Christmas and married in the March. It was quite a nice wedding, in a registry office, with a meal afterwards for close family, and a party at my husband's home in the evening for our friends. Looking back now I wish I'd had something a bit more memorable, but at the time I just wanted something quiet. I can't say I really enjoyed it very much.

We settled down to married life, living with my in-laws which was never easy with so many in the household. The pregnancy went well, I was reasonably healthy, but always seemed rather embarrassed by my condition. My son was born in the July, and then our problems really started. For the first six months he was a very difficult, demanding baby, always hungry, sleeping very little and far too much for a young couple like us to cope with alone. I can honestly say that if it hadn't been for my mother-in-law I don't think we would have been able to. She used to take him into their room sometimes at night so we could get some sleep. We were always able to get out together on our own for a night out because there was always a babysitter at home.

When my son was six months old we got a council house and it was really nice to be on our own as a family. Money was quite tight but we managed all right. I went to evening classes to do shorthand and typing so I could get a job to help out. Then things began to look up. We got a council house exchange to the area that my husband came from, opposite his parents, in fact. We still live in this house, but we have bought it now and renovated it all. Then my husband got a better-paid job.

Because of this, I didn't have to go out to work. We had our second child Nicholas who is now seven, and David who is three. Both were planned. I always said I'd had one child who wasn't planned and that was enough. I wanted my children reasonably spaced apart so I didn't have to cope with more than one baby at a time. It certainly was lovely being able to annouce to people I was pregnant without feeling any shame or embarrassment. These two were definitely easier babies to look after and I often wonder if it was because I was happier and more relaxed during the pregnancies and whether it was because I was older and better able to cope with them.

Since David arrived I felt it was time to return to studying, so I started to go to night-school. The first year I began with O-level sociology which I really enjoyed. Realising I could do other things as well as be a wife and mother gave me the confidence to get a job as a market research interviewer, which I have been doing for the past eighteen months. Last year I took the A-level sociology course and this year I am taking A-level psychology. I don't know what I'm going to do with these exams but at the moment I enjoy the challenge of doing the courses and taking the exams. At least my brain is still working after all those years at home. I am happier now than I have been for the last eleven years. I have my husband and children. I have my job and a little independence and I am continuing my education.

When I look back at myself as I was then, I think how naive I was and how immature. I thought I knew it all when in fact I knew nothing. Everything my husband and I have now we have had to struggle for. We have done everything the wrong way round and for us it has worked out fine, but it hasn't been plain sailing.

One problem with having children so young is that we never had any time alone together. We always had the children to consider. It doesn't do any marriage any good to have these sorts of responsibilities straightway. There are advantages of being young when you have your children, but these are mainly physical. Mentally it is hard to be responsible for a child when you are little more than one yourself. When I walk down the road with my eldest son now, he is nearly as tall as me and I often feel shocked that he is mine. I don't feel old enough to have a son that age and really I don't suppose I am.

As for being a friend of your child, I really don't think that is what a child wants or needs from its parents. My son was quite shocked when one of his friends asked him if I was his sister! I often say, especially if I am having a particularly trying day, that if I had my time all over again knowing what I know now, that I wouldn't marry until I was at least twenty-five, and wouldn't have children until I was thirty. At the time I didn't resent having the children and being tied down so young but now I realise that we both missed out on a lot. People often say, "Well, you'll still be young when they're off your hands." This is true enough, but my reply is, "Will we want to do the same at forty as we would have at eighteen?"

When I was seventeen I thought I'd be quite happy to settle down to married life and babies and that was about all. Now I realise that there's more to life than that. Babies grow and there has to be something else to fill your time. I know that being a housewife and mother is a worthwhile job but now it isn't enough for me.

I am also lucky that my husband is very good with the children. He is perfectly willing to look after them while I work or while I am at night-school. He helps out around the home too, cooking, cleaning, etc. I realise that nowadays this is nothing special but I do have quite a few friends whose husbands are not nearly as helpful. We both try to be as open as possible with our own children. We answer all their questions about sex as or when they arise. Just because they are boys does not mean we are going to dodge the issue of contraception. We want them to realise that it is just as much the man's responsibility as the woman's. We don't want them to make the mistake that we made. We want them to enjoy their youth and not to have the responsiblities that we had.

CONCLUSION

Having a baby when you're very young is no easy option. You gain things, and you lose things, and it's hard work. You may end up inspired and fulfilled, or overwhelmed and depressed, or up one moment and down the next. You may live each day as it comes, or make plans for the future. Every mother is different and has their own story to tell, but they share lots in common. They share the love, joy and pleasure of having a baby of their own to care for, who responds and loves them back, and makes it all seem worthwhile; at the same time they also battle against the same obstacles that society presents to them: many face unsympathetic attitudes to pregnant teenagers and teen-age mothers; they struggle to survive on social security benefits and to find somewhere decent to live and bring up their children; and they often share the experience of being let down in a relationship that they thought was true love.

Teenage mothers do not make up a huge proportion of the population, and without any personal knowledge of their lives, many people are only too ready to make unfair assumptions. If you have a child in your teens, you haven't ruined or wasted your life, and no one has the right to say this. Your live has certainly changed, however, and through the lack of facilities to help mothers of any age, this means that education and other aspirations may have to be postponed or even abandoned. There are lots of things that should be altered to improve the experience of mother-hood, and fatherhood. Childcare facilities and benefits are a crucial area which should be expanded, but are being eroded under the present government. Without these, access to education or work, or indeed any other activity, is incredibly difficult for mothers with small children. We also need more sympathetic programmes of sex education which give both girls and boys an understanding of various methods of contraception, and the confidence to obtain these and use them effectively. Using contraception does not mean you are unromantic, or a slag, it means you have a bit more control over your life and your can choose whether or not you get pregnant.

We often have little or no idea of the nature of other peoples' lives, and the emphasis in society today is on individual solutions rather than a sharing of experiences. But if the personal accounts in this book can move people and touch their hearts, if they can understand why and how girls become teenage mothers and how they feel about their babies and their lives, then it has helped to break down some of this individual isolation. After all, their lives potentially touch on those of any mother or father thinking about their own children, and anyone whose work brings them into contact with teenagers. And if you are a teenager yourself, with or without a child, I hope you have enjoyed reading about these mothers and sharing their experiences, and have gained knowledge, understanding and strength from their accounts.

USEFUL CONTACTS AND INFORMATION

Contraception

BROOK ADVISORY CENTRES
Specifically for young people. Give free contraception advice and supplies, pregnancy testing, counselling and help with social and emotional difficulties. Many Brook Centres are open fulltime, evenings and Saturday mornings.
National Office Tel: 01 708 1234

The main Brook Centres are:

Birmingham
9, York Road, Birmingham B16 9HX. Tel: 021 455 0491
City Centre Brook, Top Floor, 8–10, Albert Street,
    Birmingham B4 7UD. Tel: 021 643 5341
Handsworth Brook Centre, 102, Hamstead Road, Handsworth,
    Birmingham B19 1DG. Tel: 021 554 7553
Saltley Brook Centre, 3, Washwood Heath Road, Saltley,
    Birmingham B8 1SH. Tel: 021 328 4544

Bristol
Avon Brook Centre, 25, Denmark Street, Bristol BS1 5DQ. Tel:
    0272 292136

Coventry
Gynaecological Out-Patients, Coventry and Warwickshire
    Hospital, Stoney Stanton Road, Coventry. Tel: 0203 412627
Edinburgh
2, Lower Gilmore Place (Office), 50, Gilmore Place (Centre),
    Edinburgh EH3 9NY. Tel: 031 229 3596

London
Islington Centre, 6, Manor Gardens, London N7 6LA.
   Tel: 01 272 5599

Tottenham Court Road Centre, 233, Tottenham Court Road,
   London W1P 9AE. Tel: 01 580 2991/01 323 1522. *Ring here
   for other North and East London Centres*
Walworth Centre, 153A, East Street, London SE17 2SD.
   Tel: 01 703 9660/01 703 7880. *Ring here for other South
   London Centres*
Brixton Centre, 53, Acre Lane, London SW2 5TN.
   Tel: 01 274 4995
Merseyside
Brook Look-In, 9, Gambier Terrace, Liverpool L1 7BG.
   Tel: 051 709 4558
North East Lancashire
Brook Advisory Centres, Top Floor, 79, Church Street,
   Burnley BB11 2RS. Tel: 0282 416596

FAMILY PLANNING CLINICS
Family Planning Information Service, 27–35 Mortimer Street,
   London W1. Tel: 01 636 7866
Provide free contraception and pregnancy testing. Ring London
Information Service for details of local clinics, or look in yellow
pages, under 'Family Planning'.

Counselling

National Association for Young Person's Counselling and
   Advisory Services (NAYPCAS): 17–23, Albion Street,
   Leicester LE1 66D. Tel: 0533 554775 ex 22. Offer counselling
   and advice for young people on many issues. Ring here for
   details of local counselling services.

New Grapevine: 416, St. John Street, London EC1V 4NJ.
   Tel: 01 278 9147 (Helpline) 01 278 9157 (Office). Offers a sex
   education, information and counselling service for young
   people under 25 living in the Camden and Islington areas of
   London.

Under 21: Chestnut House, 398, Hoe Street, London E17. Tel: 01 509 1219. Counselling and information service for young people.

Family problems, adoption, fostering, mother and baby homes

Family Network Service: National Children's Home, 85, Highbury Park, London N5 1UD. Tel: 01 226 2033. Counselling service for young people and parents having problems with family life. Ring here for details of services in Birmingham, Cardiff, Glasgow, Glenrothies, Gloucester, Ilford, Leeds, Luton, Maidstone, Manchester, Norwich, Preston and Swansea.

Social services departments: Will give you information on adoption, fostering and mother and baby homes. Look for your local social services in the telephone directory.

Loneliness, depression and suicide

Samaritans: 17, Uxbridge Road, Slough, Bucks. Tel: 0753 32713. Local branches are listed in the telephone directory. 24-hour telephone service for people who are lonely, worried or feel in despair. They can refer people to other agencies for further help.

Pregnancy and abortion

British Pregnancy Advisory Services (BPAS): Austy Manor, Wootton Wawen, Solihull, West Midlands B95 6BX. Tel: 05642 3225. Offer pregnancy testing and abortion with prior counselling. They have other branches which are listed in the telephone directory.

Brook Advisory Centres – as shown above under Contraception. Offer pregnancy testing and counselling. Pregnant girls wishing to have an abortion will be referred to NHS or appropriate agency.

The Catholic church has a pregnancy agency called Lifeline which does pregnancy testing and has some accommodation in mother and baby homes. Although they offer a service to single pregnant girls, their policy is anti-abortion. No abortion advice is given and pressure may be put on girls to keep their babies. If you're pregnant and undecided what to do, and want counselling and information, it would be advisable to go to one of the other pregnancy advice centres where you will be helped to make your own decision.

Pregnancy Advisory Service (PAS): 11, Charlotte Street, London W1. Tel: 01 637 8962. Offer pregnancy testing and abortion with prior counselling. They have other branches which are listed in the telephone directory.

Womens Reproductive Rights Information Centre: 52–54, Featherstone Street, London EC1Y 8RT. Tel: 01 251 6332. Offer pregnancy testing, advice and information.

Pregnancy testing kits are available from chemist shops, and can provide a good indication of whether you are pregnant or not. However, they do vary in reliability, and if you take the test too early or do not follow the instructions correctly, they may not be accurate, so pregnancy should also be confirmed with a test done by your doctor, or at a clinic or other pregnancy advisory centre.

Single parenthood

Citizens Advice Bureaux (CAB): Myddleton House, 115–123, Pentonville Road, London N1. Tel: 01 833 2181. There is a Citizens Advice Bureau in most areas which will help with a range of issues including housing and social security, as well as legal, financial, and personal problems. Look in the telephone directory for your local CAB.

Gingerbread: 35, Wellington Street, London WC2. Tel: 01 240 0953. Self-help groups for single parent families, offering mutual support, information and advice. Ring London office for details of your local branch.

National Council for One Parent Families: 255, Kentish Town Road, London NW5 2LX. Tel: 01 267 1361. Free confidential information and advice on any problems facing a single pregnant woman or single parent, and useful booklets for single parents about issues like benefits and legal rights.

Scottish Council for Single Parents: 13, Gayfield Square, Edinburgh EH1 3NX. Tel: 031 556 3899. *Or:* 39, Hope Street, Glasgow G2 6AE. Tel: 041 221 1681

The Gillick campaign

A campaign by Victoria Gillick in 1984–1985 was initially successful in obtaining a ban on doctors giving contraceptive advice, and prescribing contraceptives to girls under sixteen without their parents' knowledge and consent. In October 1985, the House of Lords overturned this ruling. Now doctors are permitted, at their discretion, to prescribe contraceptives to under sixteen-year-old girls without their parents' consent. This means if you are under sixteen and contemplating having sex, or already having it, you can go to your doctor, or a Brook Advisory centre, or family planning clinic, where you are entitled to be given contraceptive advice and supplies. (There may be some doctors who are unsympathetic and refuse to supply contraception, if so, don't give up, go to a clinic or Brook Centre instead.)

Age of consent law

The law relating to the age of consent to sexual intercourse is contained in the Sexual Offences Act 1956, under Section 5 of which it is an absolute offence for a man to have sexual intercourse with a girl under thirteen years; and under Section 6, it is an offence for a man to have sexual intercourse with a girl aged between thirteen and sixteen years, qualified by the defence that,
(a) the man believes himself to be validly married to the girl; or
(b) he is under twenty-four and not previously charged with an offence of this kind and believes the girl to be over sixteen.
A boy under fourteen is not liable to prosecution. A girl under sixteen having sexual intercourse is not committing any offence.

NOTES

Introduction

1. In England and Wales between 1970 and 1980, the teenage pregnancy rate fell from 50 to 31 pregnancies per 1000 15–19-year-olds; the abortion rate during the same period rose from 9 to 18 abortions per 1000 15- to 19-year-olds – *Hansard*, 19 July 1983. In Scotland the teenage pregnancy rate fell from 48 to 33 pregnancies per 1000 15- to 19-year-olds from 1970 to 1980; the abortion rate increased from 5 to 11 per 1000 15- to 19-year-olds. These figures do not include Scottish women who go to England to obtain an abortion. This information together with other tables on pregnancy, birth and abortion are reproduced, in Judith Bury, *Teenage Pregnancy in Britain*, Birth Control Trust, 1984.

2. In England and Wales in 1984, the total number of teenage girls having babies was 78,755 of which 5 per cent (4,278) were under sixteen.

   In Scotland in 1985, a total of 6,518 teenage girls had babies of whom 1.8 per cent (119) were under sixteen.

   In Ireland in 1985, the total number of teenage girls having babies was 62,250, which represents 17.5 births per 1000 women.

   In Australia 1985, the total number of teenage mothers was 9,957, of whom 3 per cent were under sixteen.

   In New Zealand in 1985, the total number of teenage mothers was 4,504, of whom 4 per cent were under sixteen.

   In Canada in 1984, the total number of teenage mothers was 23,885, one per cent of whom were under fifteen.

3. OPCS Monitor, 15 July 1986.

4. For details of the law relating to the age of consent for sexual intercourse, see under Useful Contacts and Information, page 244.

5. Although initially successful, the Gillick campaign to prevent doctors prescribing contraceptives to under sixteen-year-olds was finally defeated in October 1985. This means that under sixteen-year-olds are now able to obtain contraceptive advice without their parents' knowledge or consent. See also page 244.

6. As evidenced in research such as: *Schoolgirl Mothers*, Ann-Marie Coyne, Health Education Council, Research Report No. 2; *Teenage Mothers and Their Partners*, Madelaine Simms and Christopher Smith, Institute for Social Studies in Medical Care, HMSO, 1986.; *Teenage Mothers*, Nicholas Wells, The Children's Research Fund, 1983.

1.   **Love, Boyfriends, Sex and Contraception**

1.   *Teenage Mothers and Their Partners*, Madelaine Simms and Christopher Smith, op. cit.
2.   *My Mother Said . . . The Way Young People Learned About Sex*, Christine Farrell, Routledge and Kegan Paul, London 1978.
3.   In her study of girls and sexuality, Sue Lees explores the way girls' lives are constrained by the sexual labels they may be given, such as 'slag' *Losing Out: Sexuality and Adolescent Girls*, Sue Lees, Hutchinson, 1986.
4.   *My Mother Said . . .*, Christine Farrell, op. cit.
5.   An in-depth study carried out by Isobel Allan for the Policy Studies Institute found that 96 per cent of parents and 95 per cent of their teenage children thought that schools should provide sex education: *Education in Sex and Personal Relationships*, Policy Studies Institute, 1987. A survey funded by the Health Education Council and carried out in 1985 by researchers at Exeter University in conjunction with Southampton University, found that parents of 8 to 12-year-olds said they wanted the schools to teach their children about human reproduction, conception, pregnancy and birth.
6.   The suggestion that young pregnant girls, and young mothers (and fathers) could be very effective in talking to other people of their own age about their experiences of conception, pregnancy and parenthood, is one that was also endorsed by the workers at the Arbour Project in Liverpool.
7.   Between 1974 and 1983, the overall pregnancy rate fell for both over- and under-sixteen-year-olds, but it fell much more for the older age-group. Between 1983 and 1984 it rose again, not substantially for older teenagers, but the pregnancy rate for girls under sixteen increased back to the level ten years earlier. (OPCS Monitor, 15 July 1986). This reflects more use of contraception amongst girls over sixteen which has not occurred in the younger age-group, who are generally more naive about pregnancy and how to prevent it.
8.   Bernard Ineichin, *New Community*, Vol. 12, No. 1.

3.   **School and Education**

1.   Also noted in a study of Barkerend, Pregnancy, Maternity and Education, carried out by the National Council for One Parent Families, June 1985.
2.   The advantages of attending these and other kinds of units that provide support are described and endorsed by Ann-Marie Coyne, *Schoolgirl Mothers*, op. cit.

4.   **Pregnancy and Birth**

1.   Unpublished data from Ann Cartwright's study, 'The Dignity of Labour?', Tavistock Publications, London, 1979, quoted in Madelaine Simms and Christopher Smith, op. cit.
2.   Madelaine Simms and Christopher Smith, op. cit.
3.   This was found in a survey of thirty young Afro-Caribbean women's experiences and perceptions of pregnancy and childbirth: *Black Women*

and the Maternity Services, Jo Larbie, Health Education Council, National Extension College for Training in Health and Race, 1985.

4. In the Simms and Smith study, just over two-thirds of the teenage women reported that they had suffered from depression or nerves at some time between the third and fifteenth month after giving birth.

6. Housing and Financial Survival

1. Although the official age of eligibility for council housing is eighteen, this may be waived in certain circumstances, and at the discretion of local councils. Similarly for Housing Associations, eligibility is usually seventeen-and-a-half, but this may sometimes be lowered.

2. *Wigan Pier Revisited,* Beatrix Campbell, Virago, 1984.

3. In April 1987, the government's new Social Security Act will effectively abolish the maternity grant, replacing it by a flat-rate, means-tested grant of about £75. Only those on Supplementary Benefit will be eligible for this, so this means that under sixteen-year-olds will no longer be entitled to any maternity grant at all. From April 1988, milk and vitamin tokens will no longer be available to all mothers, but again only to those receiving supplementary benefits, who have to be over sixteen. Therefore the meagre entitlements that under sixteen-year-olds have been receiving will now be taken away altogether, leaving young girls without even this small token towards the costs of motherhood.

4. According to the new Social Security Act, from April 1988, Supplementary Benefit is replaced by Income Support and the Social fund (which replaces single payments), and Family Income Supplement is replaced by Family Credit.

7. Marriage

1. Judith Bury, *Teenage Pregnancy,* op. cit.

2. Madelaine Simms and Christopher Smith, op. cit.

3. L. Rimmer, *Families in Focus: Marriage, Divorce and Family Patterns,* Study Commission on the Family, London, 1981; K. Dunnell, *Family Formation, 1976,* HMSO, 1979.

4. As found in a study by George Brown and Tirril Harris, *Social Origins of Depression: A Study of Psychiatric Disorder in Women,* Tavistock, 1978.

5. In her study of young girls, Sue Lees found that despite having a very realistic view of marriage as a domestic burden, girls saw no alternative way of obtaining security and protection, and social respectability: *Losing Out,* Sue Lees, op. cit.

10. Alternatives – Adoption and Abortion

1. *My Mother Said . . .,* Christine Farrell, op. cit.

2. A list of Brook Advisory Centres and other useful contact addresses can be found on pages 240–41.

3. Several books have been written about the contradictory feelings and emotions that many women experience after having an abortion, such as

The Ambivalence of Abortion by Linda Bird Francke, Penguin 1978; *Mixed Feelings: The Experience of Abortion* by Angela Neustetter with Gina Newson, Pluto, 1986; and *Coping with Abortion* by Alison Frater and Catherine Wright, Chambers, 1986.

11. Looking Back

1.   Feelings and experiences of being a mother with small children, and the enjoyment of gaining a separate identity outside the home through a job or some other activity, are described by many of the mothers in *Double Identity: Lives of Working Mothers*, Sue Sharpe, Penguin, 1984.